10 good choices that empower black women's lives

10

good
choices
that
empower
black
women's
lives

DR. GRACE CORNISH

crown publishers | new york

Published by Crown Publishers, New York, New York.
Member of the Crown Publishing Group.

Random House, Inc. New York, Toronto, London, Sydney, Auckland
www.randomhouse.com

CROWN is a trademark and the Crown colophon is a registered trademark of
Random House, Inc.

Printed in the United States of America.

Design by Debbie Glasserman

Library of Congress Cataloging-in-Publication Data
Cornish, Grace.
10 good choices the empower Black women's lives / by Grace Cornish.
p.   cm.
1. Afro-American women—Life skills guides.   I. Title: Ten good choices
that empower Black women's lives.   II. Title.

E185.86 .C58828   2000
305.48'896073—dc 21

00-022131

ISBN 0-609-60506-2

10 9 8 7 6 5 4 3 2 1

First Edition

**I wasn't born empowered,
but I was born to be empowered.**

Due to the fast-paced popularity of my previous book, *10 Bad Choices That Ruin Black Women's Lives,* I had to do this natural follow-up right away. It is important for you to first identify, and then release yourself from, the bad choices. Once you've done that, then let go and move onward and upward. I've tried to personally answer the hundreds of letters I've received from sisters across the country. A few are included here. For the ones I was unable to answer right away, please let this book serve as my personal letter of empowerment to you. I promise that if you make the good choices here, you will become a magnificent force to behold.

**This is dedicated to you—who've decided to empower
yourself in this lifetime.**

acknowledgments

It is truly amazing how God works. When He said, "Ask and it shall be given," He wasn't kidding. I asked to be surrounded by a group of loving, kind, and supportive people who would be a plus on my path of empowerment. And that's exactly what I got.

I have so many friends, associates, and family members to thank for their love and support. Let me start with love and appreciation for my immediate family. To Dureen McCalla, my "guardian angel" mother: Aunt D, how could I have done any of this without you? You are what unconditional love is all about. To Angelena Cornish Johnson, my sister: Ang, you are the true meaning of sisterhood—everyone should have a big sister like you. I wouldn't trade you for the world. To Clive Cornish, my father: Dads, we've come a long way, haven't we? I'm so glad you're my father. To Dena Cornish, my precious six-year-old daughter: Sweetheart, you are such a blessing and a joy. I love you more than words can explain. To Jason Johnson, my nineteen-year-old nephew: Jay, you've always been like a son to me. Stay focused and do well in life.

A special and warm message of love to Lana Cornish, my stepmother, who made the transition through God's other door while I was writing the last chapter of this book: Aunt Lana, may your soul be at peace and at one with God at this very moment. To my brothers and sisters—Zola Cornish Allen, Albert Cornish, Lanita Cornish Woodfork, Carla Cornish McPearson, Lonsley Cornish, and Chris Cornish Lopez: I love you all.

These are the key individuals that made this book possible. To Kristin Kiser, my editor at Crown: Kristin, you are dynamic! It's a pleasure working with you—I truly appreciate your keen insight and guidance. To Rachel Kahan, associate editor: Thanks for your input, and for helping to make the manuscript flow smoothly. To Janet Biehl, copy editor: Thanks for doing such a great job—the manuscript works beautifully. To Barbara Lowenstein, my agent: Barbara, I wanted a top-of-the line, first-class, no-nonsense agent—and you're it. Thanks for being so knowledgeable, straightforward, and well respected in the industry.

The remarkable folks I'm about to thank are all instrumental in my blessings and growth. To Rev. Dr. W. A. Blair: Reverend Blair, if you only knew how much your inspirational sermons and tapes have impacted and enlightened my life over the years (and across the miles). I thank God for using you as an excellent pastor, mentor, and role model. To Dr. Gwendolyn Goldsby Grant: Dr. Gwendolyn, thank you profusely; you are now officially adopted into my family. Dr. Rosie Milligan: Dr. Rosie, thanks for the pep talks throughout the years, and for taking a keen interest in my endeavors. To Helen Bungert: Helen, what can I say, but sincerest gratitude for your critique and expertise always. To Mike Millis: Mike, whoever said men and women could not be close friends without any strings attached, were certainly wrong, weren't they? I wish more brothers and sisters would have the decent, platonic, and good friendship that we do. To Connie Green: You are an excellent cousin and a supersupportive friend—thank you. To Gem Christie: Miss Gem, thank you for your guidance over the years. To Norman Hall: Thanks, Norman, for always listening and providing useful information—and above all, for always looking out for my best interest. To Lingsworth Pendley: In the Jamaican lingo, "Tank yuh, mi breda, fi yuh ongoing blessings—one love."

My acknowledgment list continues with these special individuals who have shown continued respect, love, kindness, and support for my work: Sonia Alleyne (*Black Elegance* and *Belle*), Kate Ferguson (*Today's Black Woman*), Queen Latifah (*The Queen Latifah Show*), Yanick Rice Lamb (*Heart & Soul*), Claire McIntosh (*Essence*), Pamela Johnson (*Essence*), Margena Christian (*Jet*), Sylviette McGill, (*Upscale*), Gloria Locke (*Upscale*), T. E. Alexander, Astra Austin, Ricki Lake (*The Ricki Lake Show*), Isabel Rivera (*Good Day New York*), Donnette Dunbar (*Omaha World Herald*), Jared McCallister (*The Daily News*), Hazel Smith (*The New York Beacon*), Dr. Jeff Gardere (Hit It-WLIB-FM), Monica Pierre (WQUE), Monica Harris (Black Expressions Book Club), June Zimmerman (Crown), Lindsay Mergens (Crown), Millicent L. Meeks (Runstr8t@aol.com), Monica White (Going Public, Inc.), Sister E.J. Davis (St. John M. B. Church), Carolyn Anderson (Seccess Productions), Marie Deary (Education 2000 Bookstore), Gigi Roane (Drum & Spear Books), Annette (Aframerican Bookstore), Lolita Long (*The Gleaner*), Edmund W. Lewis (*The Louisiana Weekly*), Crisena Coleman (*Just Between Girlfriends*), William July II (*Brothers, Lust and Love*), Max Rodriquez (*Quarterly Black Reviewer*), Laticia Greggs (*The Chicago Defender*), Rick Blalock (21st Century Communications), K. Thomas Oglesby (*What Black Men Must Do Now*), Patrick Riley (*BET Weekend*), Drs. Judith Sherven and Jim Sniechowski (*The New Intimacy*), and Reverend Melvin and Cassandra Tate (Mt. Lebanon AME Zion Church).

Let me put the icing on the cake and bring it home with these friends who've stood the test of time: Toni and Corey Gourdine, Heather and Alan Turnbull, Ruth and Leroy Campbell, Norma and Gilbert Lane, Jackie Moore, Liz and Mark Adorno, Margaret Grey, Marie Helen Gourage, Don Spears, Karen Seymour, Daylle Schwartz, and Rayniece Holmes.

And a great big thanks to all my readers, and to those who have allowed me to share their stories and letters in this empowerment guide.

This list is by no means complete. If I've forgotten anyone, please accept my apologies. I have no doubt that this list will definitely continue to grow as I continue to grow on God's path—"be it done to me according to my faith."

There is an old adage, "Be *careful what* you ask for, you *might just* get it." Well, here's my take on it: "Be *cheerful when* you ask, for you *will just* get it." Thank you kindly.

contents

introduction

I had to write this book. I had to write it because I've seen sisters working so hard to make it in life, yet they can't seem to get past bad memories and move ahead. I had to write it because I've seen too many sisters let bad relationships ruin their lives and let other people run their lives.

We are such beautiful and amazing women, but we've not achieved inner and outer happiness because we've been too hard on ourselves. And not only have we been too hard on ourselves, but we've also allowed others to run away with pieces of ourselves. We have given so many pieces of ourselves away to bad relationships, wrong careers, unproductive people, and societal expectations, that we're stressed out. We are stressed because we don't have enough time, energy, and appreciation left to nurture and become the lovely and empowered creatures God created us to be.

Listen, sis, one of the biggest regrets anyone can have in life is to look back and think, "I wish I had" or "I could have been." Don't let this happen to you.

The best gift you can give yourself is a balanced life—balanced among *God, health, money,* and *love.* In your hand you hold a blueprint to your personal success. This book will give you a clear vision of how we function unsuccessfully because of insecurities, negative social conditioning, and self-defeating behavior. Then it will provide the necessary tools to break free from loneliness, pain, anger, confusion, procrastination, self-pity, fear, and stress, and create a solid foundation for an empowered sense of direction, joy, success, good love, beauty, and peace of mind.

For the past ten years, I have been lecturing and facilitating self-empowerment seminars for women in business, management, government, entertainment, public relations, nursing, retailing, and recovery programs. My seminar "Self-Enhancing Secrets for Black Women" has received rave reviews. It has been successful because it focuses on creating harmony among mind, body, and spirit. I want to inspire sisters to not waste their precious time complaining about "rotten breaks," "bad luck," and "hard times," but to immediately empower their lives with the good choices I've laid out in this book. I promise that by the time you finish reading this life-enhancing guide, you'll have experienced some fantastic and amazing changes.

10 Good Choices That Empower Black Women's Lives will help you to pinpoint and create your individual sense of purpose— socially, professionally, and personally. Using anecdotes, case studies, interviews, and letters, I provide an uplifting, effective, and spiritually fulfilling program that will give you:

1. A sense of self—knowing *who* you are.
2. A sense of value—knowing *what* you are worth.
3. A sense of direction—knowing *where* you are going.
4. A sense of humor—knowing *when* to laugh.
5. A sense of belonging—knowing *how* to fit in.
6. A sense of being—knowing *why* you are important.

In many ways, life is like a lottery—you've got to play to win. But unlike the game of chance, *you can* control the draw. By facing your inner fears, getting rid of self-defeating behavior and bad relationships, loving who you are, attracting prosperity and love, and working to be the best you can be—you can't lose. The life-empowering principles in this guidebook will help bring out the winner in you. Its prescriptions and interactions will compel you to rethink what you have, to appreciate your true value—to really get in touch with and define your personal wants and needs in life—and *go for it*!

It's time to take back your power and your life—take it back from the bad relationships, bad careers, bad investments, bad company, and bad memories. It's time for you to live a fuller, happier, more productive, and wholesome life. This is your time to claim your blessings. God has given you a choice. Choose wisely, sis—choose to win, and enjoy every moment of it.

10 good choices that empower black women's lives

good choice #1

Embracing the Skin You're In

*I am black and comely . . . because the sun
hath looked upon me.*
Song of Solomon 1:5,6

Is a red rose more beautiful than a yellow one? Or a white rose prettier than a pink? Who can be the judge of which is more valuable?

Just as roses vary in their beauty, so do women. Whether white, black, Hispanic, Indian, or Asian, all are beautiful. People may have individual preferences, but to compare one type of beauty to another is simply ridiculous. There is no set standard for flowers, and there should be none for women. . . . Now, wouldn't it be great if life were a bed of roses? As we all know, this is not the case.

Several years ago, while I was a professional beauty image consultant, I presented my work in Lyons, France. My portfolio reflected a rainbow of women varying in shades, sizes, and shapes. One afternoon, while showing my portfolio to couture designer Maurice G., he remarked, "Mademoiselle Grace, I've always believed we have the most beautiful women in France, but these American women—they are very gorgeous. I think I'll move to America!"

At first I laughed because I found his expression humorous. I then thought about the underlying message and responded in a serious tone, "Monsieur G., beauty is where you look for it. All women are beautiful. With no disrespect, as a couture designer you ought to know one can find a woman's beauty by creating styles that suit her best. This enhances her natural beauty, no matter where on the globe she is located."

I cannot blame him for his thinking because he had been conditioned that way. As a mainstream designer, he was used to working with high-fashion models. He thought only these women had any claim to beauty. Can you imagine, sis? Less than one percent of the total population are selected as "models," so the remaining 99 percent can aspire to look like them. Is this nonsense or what?

This selection is made is made by a few corporations, modeling agencies, and fashion publications. The world of high-fashion modeling is a large moneymaking industry. I give these women credit for being able to succeed at it. For many young girls and women, however, the practice of having just one narrow definition of beauty causes pain, lack of self-esteem, and insecurity.

What's especially distasteful is that black women in particular are disrespected this way more than any other ethnic group in the United States. How unconscionable it is for anyone to discriminate against a certain sector of the population, just because the Creator has colored their skins with various shades of beautiful brown. Many sisters have negative feelings about their brown skin because of problems, discomforts, and false standards that Western society forces on them. Because of racial prejudice, we have undergone much suffering, oppression, and even bloodshed. But the truth is, the melanin that gives us our lovely brown tint is a magnificent chemical.

One major contributor to the self-sabotage of black women is the scarcity of self-affirming images of beautiful sisters in television and other mainstream media. In an article in *Essence* entitled, "Where Have All the Black Models Gone?" supermodel Veronica Webb wrote, "Clearly the black model is the subject of a 'disappearing act.'" Katie Ford, CEO of Ford Models, affirmed this frightening fact: "Yes, I agree that this is a totally blond season." She admitted, "It's a trend started by designers like Prada and Gucci. If you're a brunette, it's hard to get on the runway." "Think about where that left us as black models," Webb pleaded. "At least white brunettes could turn to a bottle of peroxide."

DON'T FALL FOR THE FALSE IDEAL

Fashion designers, beauty publications, and most television commercials dictate how the "ideal" woman should look: blond hair, blue eyes, white skin, pencil-thin figure, five foot seven or taller in height. The majority of women, who do not reflect these images, end up resenting themselves and wishing they looked like someone else.

This deplorable practice tells black women, "Your looks don't fit the bill—you're not good enough." While my white sisters embrace bottles of peroxide, my black sisters nurture tubes of bleaching cream. One's hair color is just an accessory, but to change one's skin color is an abomination because the chemicals in the bleaching cream actually damage and kill your natural skin cells. This is dangerous stuff, sis. Don't fall for it.

How tragically dehumanizing for another person or race to set standards for others to live by. No one has the right to criticize any of God's creations. The Creator has blessed each of us with our unique and individual features. Is man therefore greater than his Creator, to consider himself an authority on which of God's creations is ideal and which is not?

"SO CLOSE, BUT YET SO FAR"

Another feature article in *Essence*, "Hollywood Shuffle: With White Men Calling the Shots, Black Women Have No Reel Power," focused on the lack of appealing roles for black women in films today. Tyra Ferrell, an actress, shared, "I was told by an agent, 'You're talented, but you're never going to work in this town. You're too black, and in this town we like the Vanessa Williams type.' For black women in Hollywood," Ferrell concluded, "that has meant being cast at the margins as either caretaker to the white characters or as a sassy bit of exotica."

Black women have come a long way, but we still have a long way to go. Recently *Good Day New York* aired a segment on black women's self-esteem and skin-coloring issues. The program included dialogue among various professional and educated black women from ages twenty-five to sixty. The sisters chorused that low self-image is a "hidden and real pain" that black women harbor. They discussed their individual experiences, insecurities, and concerns about "keeping silent regarding ethnic features and skin complexion issues," and the harm of pretending they don't exist. They expressed an urgent need for a self-empowerment program specifically tailored to help black women overcome and heal their battles with their self-worth.

Well, this is the program, sis. I'm here to pull back the curtain of deception and let you know that there is nothing wrong, unattractive, or ugly about being black. The only thing that's wrong and ugly is *comparison*. When we compare one race to another, it damages people's minds. The practice of comparing is damaging because it psychologically binds us to a false standard of beauty created by a governing body outside of our race. Many black women have become discontented and depressed, silently wishing to look more like society's ideal, and as a result, they have adopted body image and beauty standards within our very own race.

It's healing time. Let's get to the healing by facing, erasing, and replacing the false beauty ideal. It's time to stop pretending. The only way to erase this type of false programming is to acknowledge it, analyze it, and disregard it. If you have a wound on your foot and do not treat it, doesn't the affliction become widespread? If you bandage it, cover it up, because you are ashamed of people seeing it, won't the disease continue to fester until you eventually lose your foot? But if the wound is exposed and properly treated, so what if people see it? Isn't it better to see it and heal it?

GIVE YOURSELF PERMISSION TO LOVE YOUR PACKAGE

It's healing time, sis. It's time to stop grinning and bearing our internal pain—time to stop pretending or aspiring to be something other than what we are—beautiful melanic women. God does not make mistakes. If He wanted you to be another color besides beautiful black in this lifetime, He would have created you in that particular image. If He wanted you big-busted or small-busted, pencil thin or pleasingly plump, tall or petite, He would have molded you thus.

Enough is enough. It's time to get rid of the ancient, fossilized mentality that says, "Don't air your dirty laundry out in public." Too many sisters are crying behind closed doors. They are in pain. (So are my brothers, but that's a whole different book.) Some of the worst feelings you can have as a woman are to feel unattractive, disrespected or less than ideal. What's even more disturbing is that we ourselves have set a complexion standard within our own race. How very unfortunate.

HOW DARE WE DISGRACE ANOTHER SISTER'S FACE!

When supermodel Alec Wek, a richly melanic, deeply dark-skinned sister with strong African features, made history by being the first black woman to be featured on the cover of *Elle,* her looks were verbally whiplashed by members of the black community. They said many unkind things about this sister that made her feel rejected, including the term "savage-looking." In a magazine interview, this dynamic sister shared, "It hurts to not be accepted by my own people." How disgusting and deplorable of those limited-thinking, narrow-minded, self-loathing, self-appointed critics. Good grief, sis, how bad have we gotten? Instead of being glad for this sister and her accomplishments, we tore her apart. We need a strong dose of unity in the sister-community. But we'll talk about that later.

I want to say that I am so proud of sister Alec, and I felt such joy when *Essence* paraded her on its cover. I was just as pleased when Oprah featured her on her show. Oprah warmly embraced our sister and said, "If you were on the magazine covers when I was growing up, it would have prevented a lot of my self-esteem problems."

Way to go, sister Alec—keep on keeping on. And for any sister reading this, no matter what your individual package is, from the darkest to the lightest, thinnest to the plumpest, shortest to the tallest—you keep on keeping on also, and don't let anyone fool you into believing that you're less than ideal.

National studies show that black women are more accepting and confident with varying body sizes than our white sisters. The pencil-thin model isn't the black standard of beauty. Let's face facts: Nature has designed black sisters with varying degrees of voluminous body parts—especially the behinds. But negative psychological programming about skin coloring leads to depression and other emotional dysfunctions. One black author, in her book about depression, stated that when she was younger, she was teased and taunted by the white kids in her class as "ugly monkey." Another said that as a child, she wished desperately that she had been born white and believed that if she brushed against her white classmates, their skin coloring would somehow rub off on her. So she went around brushing her arm against the arms of as many white kids as she could.

The root of these women's depression (and even suicide attempts) sprouted from early negative conditioning and poor self-image.

Let's Get to the Root to Find the Remedy

Just where do we get our early programming and role models? One day while driving back to New York City after I led a women's weekend retreat, my sister-friend Ruth and I were discussing the impact of my seminar. Our conversation turned to the importance of emptying out all our negative childhood memories. Ruth shared with me what she had discovered two years ago through her nineteen-year-old daughter Isis. Like so many parents, she had had no clue how mainstream cartoons, storybooks, and fairy tales influence our self-esteem as black women until she read an essay that Isis had written at seventeen for a high school project. The following is a portion of this remarkable essay. It is so awesome that I have to share it with you:

Every minute of the day, young girls are being told fairy tales that will instill beliefs and values in them forever. As I grew up, I can remember that fairy tales meant a lot to me. For most kids, their childhood is spent role-playing. I used to watch Disney movies like *Cinderella* and *Sleeping Beauty* over and over again. No matter how many times I saw the movies, every time they seemed new and foreign to me. Then came my dreams—I wanted to *be* Cinderella and Sleeping Beauty. They were the epitome of beauty. They both consisted of hair as golden sun, skin as white as snow, lips as red as roses, and eyes as blue as the sky. My reality was that I had none of these "magnificent" traits. My hair is as black as ebony, my skin is brown like honey, my lips are the color of cinnamon, and my eyes are as brown as deep mahogany. There was no comparison, no medium, no anything. My reality was that I was different, ugly, and black.

I can remember sometimes cursing God, because he made me different. I wondered, Why me? Why couldn't I have at least one of Cinderella's "great" characteristics? Just one. I wanted to do anything to change myself, from taking a magic potion, to scrubbing myself to death, or bleaching my skin. Even though everyone who was around me was black, I never realized that we were the same. I thought I alone was different. To me there was no black race, just Cinderella and Sleeping Beauty versus Isis.

Throughout my childhood there was very rarely a heroine who possessed my traits. Even my "black" Barbie looked white. She had a straight nose, thin lips, and straight hair. Everywhere I looked, there was another model to compare myself to. Then after I left my all-black and Hispanic public school, I met her. She was beautiful. She had long golden hair, sky blue eyes, and snow white skin. Her name was Madison, and she was loved by everyone. I could not believe it— Cinderella was *real!* This made things worse. Now I had a living, breathing person to compare myself to. She had been created in the fairy tales, developed in my mind, and now she was real! At this moment, I was able to see all of my differences, mishaps, and faults—up close and personal. I began to hate her and myself. I hated her not because she was mean or nasty to me, but because society had told me that I was supposed to look like her and *be* her. The big problem with society's request was that I wasn't anything like her—that's why I hated myself. In school we were taught how to act, talk, and be smart. These were aspects where Madison and I were equal, but nowhere else.

YOU BECOME WHAT YOU'VE BEEN TAUGHT

. . . I have witnessed this instance several times with my four-year-old niece, Asia, who is Cinderella's, Sleeping Beauty's and the Little Mermaid's biggest fan. She knows exactly how to work the VCR, and as soon as Cinderella comes on, she is singing the score. Even though she knows the entire line, she is glued to the television as if she has never seen the movie before. She reacts to everything that takes place and totally identifies with Cinderella, who in the Disney version is a young beautiful [white] maiden.

After the tale ends, my niece plays out the entire story, adding her own twists and ad-libs. The effect of the movie then begins. Asia immediately runs around collecting her tools to begin role-playing. She gets a wig, some makeup, and some kind of dress. She paints her lips red and powders her face with *baby powder*. She realizes that she can do nothing to change her hair color, so she decides that she will play the "ugly" stepsister. The stepsisters are usually portrayed with dark hair and eyes, and they are continuously referred to as ugly.

As she plays the part of the stepsister, she slowly transforms into her most desired part of Cinderella. She does this in a sly and sneaky way, as if she will be punished for not continuing to play the stepsister.

FAIRY TALES MUST BE MONITORED FOR CHILDREN OF COLOR

... Many people believe that fairy tales are harmless and offer great positive values to children. Fairy tales may have their good points because they help children to differentiate between character types, but why are certain characteristics identified with certain characters? In these tales the good people are considered beautiful because of their blond hair, white skin, and blue eyes—while evil is identified with dark olive-colored skin, dark hair, dark eyes and sometimes old age. In the olden days when these tales were created, this was acceptable because the population was fully Caucasian. People of color were considered taboo [because] the people were afraid of the unknown. For them these idols worked, but what about the people of color?

In today's American society, where nothing is sacred, why haven't these figures been changed to reflect most of the population? Kids see hundreds of different cultures in one day— but when they read their favorite fairy tale, one culture is featured.

Eventually children affected by fairy tales will grow up and experience many different problems, big and small. They will have low self-confidence and self-esteem. They will feel inferior and jealous toward "beautiful" women; they will feel hatred toward their bodies and looks. They will try dieting, makeovers, plastic surgery, and numerous other body-altering fads to change their already-beautiful bodies. They will spend billions of dollars on straightening their hair, bleaching their skin, wearing color contacts, and doing other things to help make them look white or avoid looking black. They will eventually realize that they hate themselves and their lifestyles for no obvious or apparent reason, except their "invented" reasons.

YOU'VE GOT TO CREATE BALANCE

When my mother eventually realized what was happening to me, she intervened and expressed to me how beautiful I am. She enrolled me in an array of classes from dance to drama. She figured that they would help build my confidence and break me out of my shell of shyness. She took me to "thousands" of cultural events to show me beautiful black people at their best of everything. She bought me and my other affected friends "real" black dolls and read us the black fairy tale books that had black faces we could be proud of and relate to. Some of them were slightly changed, but the point was the heroines and heroes were kids of color.

I was still able to watch Disney movies, as long as my mother had created a balance for me. She never realized that my self-hatred had stemmed from the tales; but she knew that the world consisted of many cultures and that children need and should be exposed to every last one of them—especially their own. As I have matured, my reality changed: I realized that I am beautiful, black, and powerful.

Amen, Isis! Isn't this young sister amazing? She is presently enrolled at Howard University and will no doubt be a beacon of light into many people's lives.

IT'S NOT WHAT YOU HAVE, BUT HOW YOU WORK WITH WHAT YOU'VE GOT

Sis, let me share with you the most important beauty tip you'll ever need to know: *The key to being beautiful is to enjoy being yourself. For your beauty is as individual as you are.*

Have you ever wondered why some women who are far outside the so-called "beauty ideal" are considered beautiful while others are not? However varied their appearance may be, there is something about them that is undeniably appealing. What do they possess that makes men desire them and other women admire them?

These sisters have discovered how to effectively do the best with what they have been naturally blessed.

You too must do what suits you best, sis. When corporations advertise the "ideal look," they are selling a product that the model is either wearing or representing. To get you to make the purchase, they have to convince you that the model represents beauty and that you can be beautiful too, if only you would wear or eat what she wears or eats. It's a selling gimmick—a basic marketing technique. And it works.

It works because approximately ninety-five out of one hundred women make the same mistake. They imitate each other's styles too closely. They copy hairstyles, makeup, and clothing. These important assets should all be chosen on an individual basis, with a view to bringing out the very best in each individual woman. Everyone is structured differently.

Beauty cannot be cultivated by copying another. Instead of wondering, "Why couldn't I have been born with _____?" start asking, "What can I do to improve my _____?"

When you learn to be truly pleased with who you are, you emit a certain force field that draws others to you. This is what is known as charisma or magnetic attraction. It's a very important aspect of beauty that most people overlook. Beauty in its totality is threefold. The three segments of complete beauty are:

1. Mind beauty—thinking good
2. Body beauty—looking good
3. Soul beauty—feeling good

These three aspects are interrelated. If any one of them is negative, the other two will be affected. The opposite holds true as well. If you can make one aspect positive, the other two will soon follow.

MIND BEAUTY—THINKING GOOD

We are familiar with the saying, "When you look good, you feel good." It has a lot of truth to it. But more importantly, when you *feel* good about yourself, you *look* even better.

Beauty originates from within. What you think is what you become. Plant the seeds of confidence in your mind. A positive affirmation grafted onto your mind will grow positively; a negative one will bring about defeating results.

Accept and love yourself as you are now. Do the best with what the Creator has blessed you with. One of the major concerns of black women is the length and texture of their hair. A lot of sisters are victims of the "good hair versus bad hair" mentality in the black community. If you feel your hair is "too nappy" or "too short," you can always braid it, relax it, or weave it, *if you choose to do so*. Remember, hair is an accessory—you can always change it. It's merely a part of your body's package, but not the true essence of who you are. Your state of mind is what defines who you are. You can change a specific thing about yourself without being unkind to yourself.

Suppose you feel your hips are too big, or that you weigh too much. It's okay to dislike the fat on your body without disliking your body or yourself. Recite positive affirmations to yourself: "I love who I am, but I don't like the extra weight on my body. I grow more and more lovely each day, and I exercise and eat right to keep my body healthy."

"A Mind Is a Terrible Thing to Waste"

We have to form honorable and kind individual relationships with ourselves. Sis, pay attention to the words you utter to and about yourself. For example, a lot of black women suffer from dry and ashy skin. During one of my workshops, Valarie complained that she experienced severe itching all over her body right after every shower. The itching would last from ten to fifteen minutes. She said she visited a few dermatologists in the past, but the problem always returned after a few short weeks of relief. Her exact words were "Sometimes my skin itches me so badly that I feel that I'm losing my mind."

"Be careful of the words you utter, sis," I informed her. "It's not your skin that's itching you, but rather something that's itching your skin. When you say your skin's itching you, you're relating a negative affirmation to your mind that your skin is doing something bad to you. The reason you feel as if you're going out of your mind is because subconsciously the negative affirmation tells your mind that your skin is tormenting you—and in retaliation, you probably scratch as if there's no tomorrow."

"You're right," she confirmed. "You know, the more I scratch, the more it seems to itch. And it just keeps on and on, as if it won't stop. Yuugghh!"

"I'm sure it's frustrating, sis," I comforted. "The first thing you have to do is take it out of your mind that your skin itches you. It doesn't. Something itches your skin—it could be the harshness of the water, or the bath products that you use. You have to get at peace with yourself. Tell yourself that you love your skin and you will not let anything itch it or harm it. Try this from now on: Use a moisturizing body wash to bathe your skin, and above all implant positive affirmations in your mind. Keep repeating 'I'm at peace with myself. I feel comfortable in my body temple. My skin is healthy and beautiful, and I love who I am.'"

Five months after our conversation, Valarie called to report that she had been "happily itch-free for four months, and still did her positive affirmations."

YOUR MIND IS A DIVINE MACHINE—OPERATE IT WISELY

Sis, throw out all your negative images. Clean your mental house. Today, right now, remove all negative images and habits. Good internal characteristics contribute much to mind beauty. Friendliness, kindness, and honesty are the basic components. Be your own best friend. Think on the nice things about you. Develop a pleasant personality toward yourself and others.

Visualize your mind as your personal safe-deposit box. Only you possess the key to open or close it. You are the only person who decides what gets put in or taken out. Put positive thoughts and memories into your safe-deposit box.

Develop the habit of bringing in the good choices and throwing out the bad choices. Keep positive thoughts in your mind as often as possible. Sis, your thoughts are the only things you have total control over. No one else can get into your mind, unless you let them.

The Universal Law "As a man thinketh, so he is" is quite true. The woman who thinks she's unattractive becomes more unattractive; the woman who thinks she is beautiful becomes more beautiful.

DARE TO ASSERT YOUR OWN BEAUTY

If people would stop worrying about whether they look good enough to other people, they would be more contented with themselves. Let me use a sister I know very well for this example:

Gladys L. is a professional singer. She is very attractive and very much in the public eye. She is very mindful of her appearance. She wears exquisite clothing and jewelry. Heads turn when she enters a room. Externally Gladys L. is a very beautiful person, but internally is a different story. She is so concerned about what people think of her looks that she actually neglects to consider what she herself thinks of her looks.

She does not enjoy her good looks. Onstage and offstage, she spends most of her time worrying about what other people think about her physical appearance. Onstage is understandable, but offstage is outrageous. She has very little self-confidence. Because of her insecurity, she tends to be abrupt with people. Once people get to speak with her, they find her personality unattractive. This unnecessary negativity could be prevented if she would use positive affirmations to boost her self-esteem and internal beauty. It's ironic—while she worries about how she appears to others, other people worry about how they appear to her.

The moral in grassroots ebonics: If it ain't happening inside, it ain't gonna last outside.

The majority of women are concerned about how others judge their beauty. They wonder, "Do I look good enough?" Stop and ask yourself, "Good enough by whose standards?" Learn a lesson from the old saying "Beauty is in the eye of the beholder." Observe your own beauty. Set your own standards. Learn to respect your thoughts. Don't feed the negative doubts; let them die of starvation.

Govern your beauty by your own thinking, not by the thoughts of others. Let them worry about their own looks. Nor should you judge another person's beauty by your own standards. Each person, like you, has her own individual beauty.

The quicker you acknowledge and practice this, the happier and more peaceful you'll feel and look. Tell yourself, "I am beautiful. I am the most beautiful person I know. I'm not necessarily the prettiest, the most physically fit, or the most dynamic, but I'm certainly the most beautiful." Repeat this until it becomes a natural part of your thinking.

Your beauty is the totality of all the characteristics you possess. Once you have successfully cultivated your inner beauty, it will naturally show externally—in your posture, your walk, your social mannerisms, even your facial expression.

A pleasant face is a lovely sight. A smile alone creates a delightful appearance. It draws people to you. Believe in your good qualities and share them with others. Help them to enjoy your presence. Think, "I am a winner, I am a lovely beautiful creation of God," and you truly shall be.

BODY BEAUTY—LOOKING GOOD

Looking good is important. Your appearance influences your lifestyle, your friendships, your relationships, and even your career.

The pressure to look good, whether openly stated or silently implied, is very real. It is said, "You can't judge a book by its cover." But that is just what people do. When we attend a social function, we dress the part. Whether you go to a business meeting, a cocktail party, or a date, it is important to look your best. For you will be judged. For most people, the first impression is a lasting one. This may not be fair, but it is true.

This book will prepare you for what's out there. It will help you to set your own pace and become your best self. Human beings are judgmental creatures. It is our nature to evaluate and compare. You will be judged, fairly or unfairly, by your appearance.

Most black women are severe critics of their own looks. They compare themselves to magazine pictures, television images, and other women, and they believe they fall short. They do not realize that most of these images are the result of proper makeup and lighting. By comparing themselves to these models, they are unfairly judging themselves.

Sis, the pictures in fashion magazines are retouched and airbrushed several times. The pictures on TV and movie screens are enhanced by makeup and lighting. The images are just that, images, not reality, either for you or for the models themselves. You can never become them, nor should you want to; you have your own unique package. They are just doing their job. They should be respected for their skill at expressing their own beauty. By all means, admire other people's beauty. But don't worship it. And don't neglect your own.

CHOOSE TO DO THE BEST WITH WHAT YOU'VE GOT

Several years ago, while I was still engaged as a beauty image consultant, I represented some major cosmetics companies. I targeted the New York and London markets. I consulted thousands of women about their beauty, makeup, and skin care.

I was amazed by the number of women who are dissatisfied with their looks. Most women do not like the way they look—women of all races, ages, complexions, sizes, and intellectual backgrounds. All had one thing in common: lack of appreciation for their appearance, especially their skin coloring. While my black sisters were buying the bleaching formulas, my white sisters were purchasing the tanning ones.

There were so many complaints, it would take an entire book to address all of them. Everyone wanted to look like someone else. All were deprived of the joy of loving themselves.

"ACCENTUATE THE POSITIVE, ELIMINATE THE NEGATIVE"

Every woman has the potential to be beautiful. We all must learn the right type of makeup and clothing to wear—the right way to enhance our own beauty. Let's start with the basics.

There is no basic "flaw" that cosmetics cannot counter. Your makeup should be carefully selected to match your individual skin complexion and texture. It should not be worn as a mask or a shield to hide behind.

It should be properly applied to accentuate and bring out your natural beauty. Any good makeup artist should be able to guide you. Go to a beauty salon, or check out the cosmetics counter at your local department store. Try many different cosmetics before selecting one as your own. Many large department stores offer complimentary makeovers; ask for one.

Make sure you ask for a trained makeup artist and skin-care specialist to work with you. All cosmetics attendants should be experienced in this area, but some are cosmetics salespersons, not specialists.

Take a friend with you to provide a second opinion. Many women go to cosmetics outlets and are convinced by an attendant to purchase a product, but once home, the look seems different. They try the product for a few days, thinking they need time to get used to it. They get negative reactions from their friends and families. They then realize that the product is not right for them.

The product ends up being thrown away or stored in the medicine cabinet, never to be used again. These women have wasted valuable time, energy, and money. Sadly, they may blame their own looks for the "failure," losing faith in their ability to enhance their natural beauty, all because of misinformation.

A good makeover can open many doors for you. A properly made-up woman carries an air of prosperity. She is sought after, both personally and professionally. Ask any professional model what her most important tool is. Why not attract others by using a few cosmetics that will enhance your best features? I've outlined a set of practical, useful, easy, and complete step-by-step beauty tips in Chapter 2 of *Radiant Women of Color.*

IS YOUR BODY SPEAKING THE RIGHT LANGUAGE?

Have you ever seen a man eagerly open a door for one woman but ignore others? Or a salesperson gladly acknowledge one customer with a vibrant "Hello, ma'am, how can I help you?" but disregard another? Or a supervisor whose instructions are harmoniously carried out by her employees, while another supervisor is only grudgingly obliged?

These women have the "it" quality that makes them stand out strikingly, no matter how varied their appearance. They get the "Yes, ma'am" treatment instead of the "Hey, gal." They command respect, confidence, and admiration. These are the sisters who have learned how to dress to impress. They know it's not what they wear that counts, but how well they wear it.

Your appearance tells people about you. Make sure it makes positive statements. Check your appearance carefully before you leave your home. It costs very little to be clean and neat. It always pays to dress properly. Use clothing as an aid to build your confidence.

Your appearance has a significant effect on your thinking. A nurse feels most nurturing when she is in uniform; a woman feels most like an executive when she is dressed like one. She feels sexier when she is dressed sensuously.

I was at a networking party at a black business expo recently. I couldn't believe the tight, ill-fitting, revealing "hoochie mama" outfits that some of our sisters were wearing at this black-tie event. There is a time and place for everything. There is a big difference between dressing sexy and dressing sleazy.

It was obvious that the women wore the extremely skintight, body-revealing attire in hopes of attracting businessmen. It's okay to go for high-rolling venture capitalists and entrepreneurs if that's your preference, sis, but do it with style. Keep in mind that a lot of men who attend these expos are in town only for a night or two and are only looking for a quickie or a one-night stand. If you dress cheaply, you will be treated as a tart to be toyed with. Carry yourself with dignity and respect. If you want a businessman, sis, then dress businesslike. Carry yourself with dignity and respect. You can be businesslike, classy, and attractive at the same time without having to reveal your body parts. Enough said.

MAKE SURE YOUR "WRAPPING" IS RIGHT ON THE MONEY

As discussed earlier, your physical exterior and mental interior are intertwined with the emotional center of your soul. They directly affect each other. When you look good outside, you feel better inside.

At a fruit and vegetable market one day, I looked at a section that had red plums marked at $1.99 a pound. In another section, what looked like exactly the same red plums were wrapped in plastic and priced at $2.49 a pound. I asked one of the cashiers to tell me the difference between the plums at $1.99 a pound and those at $2.49 a pound.

"The only difference," she replied, "is the plastic covering. People buy three times as many wrapped plums because they think they look nicer that way."

Keep the plum example in mind the next time you are marketing yourself. Properly "wrapped," you have a better opportunity to sell your presentation. The simple fact is: The quantity of public acceptance you receive is based on the quality of your "wrappings."

Take a look around you. Notice the woman who is shown the most courtesy and respect in stores, at work, and in restaurants. Her well-groomed appearance, upright posture, and brisk walk tell people, "I am important. I am prosperous, confident, and intelligent. I can be trusted. I respect myself; therefore you will respect me."

The sloppily dressed female's appearance says, "I don't think much of myself. I am unimportant, careless, and not doing well. I don't deserve special treatment; I am used to being overlooked."

DRESS FOR SUCCESS WITHOUT BREAKING YOUR BANK

In training programs I emphasize that women should dress successfully to complement their personality. In response, I'm sometimes told, "I'm ready to better my appearance, but how can I afford the kind of clothes I need without going broke? I would have to wear top designer clothing to look successful."

Many women mistakenly believe that they cannot look successful unless they wear designer clothing. Let me explain some facts about designer clothing.

Each season many new fashions and trends are introduced into the market. A small circle of top designers decides which colors, styles, and fabrics will be the season's theme. The selected styles are then shown to clothing buyers and fashion reporters. They are placed in fashion publications for consumers to absorb. They are then made available to the general public in clothing stores.

New York City, the fashion capital of the world, is one large runway with an ongoing fashion show. Every day you can see thousands of consumers who are products of fashion statements, fashion disasters, or just plain questionable fashions. A few years ago I attended a women's empowerment seminar with a business associate in midtown. One of the speakers was a woman dressed in a designer-style swing-trapeze jacket. The fabric was tastefully color-blocked in three bright colors. She wore a black miniskirt to complement this design. Her hair was done in a flip hairstyle.

My associate remarked, "Doesn't she look nice? Everything flows together—her hair, her makeup, and her clothing." I agreed wholeheartedly.

After the seminar, on our way to a restaurant, I noticed a woman wearing the same designer fashion as the one we had admired earlier. I asked my associate what she thought about this woman's attire. She replied, "What a disaster! Didn't she look in the mirror before she left home?"

It's unfortunate but true, sis—it did look frightful. The outfit did not suit the woman's shape. But the designer fashion we were both finding so unpleasant was the same one we had admired earlier. The difference was the fit—that's all.

• *The problem:* Many women copy each other's styles of dressing. They imitate someone who is several inches shorter or taller or who weighs several pounds more or less. But the look they admired so much on the other woman does not work for them.

- *The solution:* Think about what's best for your body structure. What is suitable for another woman may not be suitable for you. Select your wardrobe on the basis of the color, style, and fabric that complement your body structure.

WHAT'S IN A NAME?

Your clothing should enhance your natural physique. Many people incorrectly assume that the more expensive the clothing, the better the fit. Many buy clothing because of the name on the label. They assume that if they wear a famous brand name, they are making a fashion statement. But if the garment doesn't suit their frame, they become fashion disasters instead.

Although many designers make some fabulous garments, don't get hypnotized by the brand-name phenomenon. Some designer clothing is made by the same factories as some lesser-known names. The only difference is the label, the price tag, and the market campaign affixed to a designer clothing line. Many times we pay a high price for wearing the designer's name, instead of for the quality of the garment itself.

Make sure you know the history of designers before purchasing their labels. It is reported that a mainstream designer blatantly declared on the Oprah Winfrey show, "I do not make my clothes with 'minorities' in mind." Firstly, that designer is out of order and insulting. Secondly, don't force your frame into a garment that may be cut too narrow in the hips for your body type. Tight-fitting clothes interfere with your blood circulation. Why sacrifice your health and hard-earned money for certain undeserving designers? Support the designers who are decent and smart enough to create garments with *all* women in mind.

Go for the gold—you're too beautiful to shortchange yourself.

Put Fit before Fashion

Some women get trapped by the "sale syndrome." If an item is on sale, no matter how ghastly it may be, they buy it. They compromise proper fit for the discounted price. They rationalize, "This is a good price. It doesn't fit perfectly, but it doesn't look too bad on me. Anyway, girl, at this price, I can't pass it up."

Sis, sales are terrific! Which woman doesn't enjoy purchasing her wardrobe at a discounted price? But whether your price range is budget, moderate, or high-fashion, you should *put fit first*. Whether a dress costs ten, a hundred, or a thousand dollars, make sure it looks good on you. If it doesn't, don't buy it.

If you want to be successful, start dressing successfully now. Don't make the mistake of thinking, "I'll dress successfully after I become successful." This is a big mistake. Your goal is to stand out from the crowd. Be distinctive in your dressing. Bring out the winner that you are, sis. You'll project leadership in a silent, dignified, and unmistakable manner.

Quality Beats Quantity

Let your dressing reflect wealth. The expensive look need not cost a lot of money. One of the secrets of power dressing is to pay twice the amount but purchase half as much. Remember and apply this every time you shop for dresses, blouses, suits, shoes, lingerie, coats, scarves—everything in your wardrobe.

To the well-dressed sister, quality is more important than quantity. It's better to invest in your wardrobe by buying a few good pieces than by buying a closetful of mediocre clothing. Don't be penny wise and pound foolish in your appearance. You'll be better off financially because:

1. You'll get more pleasure from your garments. Better clothes always stay in style longer.

2. "Quality" always lasts twice as long. You'll get twice the wear that you would from an inferior product.

3. You'll get better service and advice from a sales associate who is selling a fifty-dollar dress than from one selling a ten-dollar dress.

Sis, make sure your appearance tells the world, "I am a woman who is special. I am beautiful. I should be treated that way." Remember, your outside beauty enhances your inside beauty, while your inside beauty empowers your outside looks.

SOUL BEAUTY—FEELING GOOD

Now that you've learned the secrets of thinking and looking beautiful, it's time to master feeling beautiful.

Soul beauty is probably the most difficult to obtain because it's the simplest. People tend to gravitate to the more difficult things in life. The sublevels of the three forms of beauty are *wanting, doing,* and *being.* Let me explain:

1. Mind beauty is *wanting* to be beautiful and thinking of ways to accomplish it.

2. Body beauty is *doing* what is necessary to improve your external looks.

3. Soul beauty is *being* beautiful, by simply knowing and accepting it.

Have faith in your beauty. You desired it, you have worked on it. Now it's time just to feel it. *Believing you are beautiful causes you to be beautiful.* Reread this a couple of times, and let it sink in.

To help you develop the habit of feeling beautiful, continuously repeat to yourself, "I feel beautiful." This will give you more effective results than merely saying, "I am beautiful." For feeling is greater than wanting. When you feel something, you already know it. The emotion of feeling beautiful stimulates an inner peace and keen sense of worth. This causes being beautiful to be integrated into your system. It becomes an automatic expression of you.

Feelings coupled with thoughts, whether positive or negative, harness remarkable power. That's why it's so important for you to allow only positive thoughts to live in your mental house. You are the owner and the landlord of this property called your mind. You have the right to evict negative thoughts and to keep them from moving back in. Meditate on this often.

You now have the formula for being beautiful. You are no longer misinformed, sis; you are now well informed. Decide just how beautiful you want to be, and be it!

DEVELOP A BEAUTY CONTRACT WITH YOURSELF

Form a Beauty Contract with yourself about how you will enjoy being a beautiful person. This should consist of:

1. Your personal definition of *beautiful*—what it means to you as an individual.

2. An "I feel beautiful because _____" list. You can write as many items as you like, but six should be your minimum. You may update and revise your affirmations as often as you desire. Do it six days a week until you are quite comfortable with your beauty. Remember to include both your internal and external qualities.

3. A pledge to yourself with your signature.

IT'S OKAY TO TOOT YOUR OWN HORN

Below is an example of my personal Beauty Contract, with my own definition of *beautiful*. I've shared it with numerous sisters, and it worked quite well for hundreds of them. If you feel like using it as part of your own, enjoy. But keep in mind the importance of forming your own individual concept of what it means to be beautiful—which you truly are, sis. Go for it!

BEAUTY CONTRACT

BEAUTIFUL—The state of being pleased with one's mental, physical and emotional wholeness . . . The peaceful completeness of one's mind, body, and soul . . . Joyous acceptance of the me, myself, and I . . . bringing out the best in me.

Affirmations

1. I feel beautiful because I have pretty brown skin.
2. I feel beautiful because I am guided and protected in every way by Divine powers.
3. I feel beautiful because I made someone feel good about herself today.
4. I feel beautiful because I took a relaxing bubble bath today.
5. I feel beautiful because my new outfit looks terrific on my body.
6. I feel beautiful because I'm alive and healthy.

I ____(name)_____ feel I am the most beautiful person I know. I respect and enjoy my total beauty. I respect the beauty of others as well. Every day I grow more beautiful. Thank God for my unique body temple.

_____(signature)_____

A LITTLE VANITY GOES A LONG WAY

King Solomon advised wisely in Ecclesiastes 9:7–9, "Let thy garments always be white; and let thy head lack no ointment. Live joyfully with whom thou lovest all the days of the life of thy vanity; for that *is* thy portion in *this* life."

Speaking of "living joyfully with love," let's proceed to the next chapter.

good choice #2

Accepting "Better Love," Not "Bitter Love"

If two lie together, then they have heat;
but how can one be warm alone?

Ecclesiastes 4:11

As a woman in this society, you've been conditioned from birth to become a wife. You've been told to act like a lady and that someday Prince Charming will come along to rescue you. He will sweep you off your feet and take care of you, and you will live happily ever after.

It is therefore natural for you to want an ideal mate to love, appreciate, and cherish you. Many sisters are involved in happy relationships and marriages, but unfortunately, many more are not. A large number are still waiting for the promised fairy-tale romance to materialize. Others have given up hope of ever finding their prince and have settled for the court jester instead. Many have compromised their ethics and have resorted to having an affair with someone else's mate. Still others have chosen celibacy to escape the hurt felt when Prince Charming turns out to be Prince Harming.

Statistics compiled from my national seminars show that at present, only two out of every twenty women consider their relationship to be fulfilling. Three out of every five couples divorce each year. This is a very frightening number. But do not let it discourage you from looking for and finding your ideal mate. Many people are easily discouraged by the "bad" relationships in their past. If you choose wisely, you won't end up being one of life's negative love statistics. Life is an ever-evolving experience. Don't surrender. It's fine to learn from the past, but don't dwell there. A loving relationship is a most rewarding one; it should not be avoided for fear of being hurt again.

There are many reasons for an unsuccessful relationship. Although you're not responsible for the actions of a mate, you are responsible for your own.

DON'T SELL YOURSELF SHORT

A primary reason for love gone bad is that all too often we sell ourselves short, because we don't believe in our own ability.

Most people have more respect for others than they do for themselves, even for those who lead them astray. We quickly hand over our hearts and lives to others who may not be qualified to run their own lives, much less ours. Sis, you have got to remember to "check them out before you let them in."

When you've formed a strong bond with yourself, no one can rock your foundation. Remember the term that has been drilled into us from Sunday school, "Love thy neighbor as thyself"? This is such a precious statement, it has been labeled Divine. Love is the most powerful emotion of all. But before you can honestly love another, you must first learn to love yourself.

To cultivate love for yourself, you must appreciate your individuality. Imagine, no two people are exactly alike. No two people think or act precisely alike. So who's to say who is more valuable in a relationship? When you really think about it in depth, it is fascinating that there's only one unique you in this world. You are original, sis.

Most people don't acknowledge this special quality about themselves. They haven't been taught how. Learning to appreciate your uniqueness is your first step toward being fully yourself.

At many points in our lives, we are all diamonds in the rough. Sometimes the process of cutting away the debris, of discovering, developing, shaping, and polishing our true worth, involves a great deal of pain.

This letter comes from an on-line reader:

Dear Dr. Cornish,

I read your book *10 Bad Choices That Ruin Black Women's Lives*. I seem to have found myself in chapters 4, 5, 6, and 7. I noticed that as I went on and on in those pages, it became harder and harder to read. I was reading some of the most painful and revealing parts of my life. Although those "situations" are over, your book helped me to take an honest look at myself and my relationships. I now feel as though I am beginning to truly heal my inner scars. Thank you, and keep the work you are doing going.

This sister has made a major breakthrough on her personal path of healing. Although it was painful, she made a good choice by not giving up—she has taken a fascinating journey to self-discovery. For years she had traveled with her excess baggage stuffed with emotional turmoil. The pain she felt was from examining and emptying her overloaded suitcase. This courageous sister is now ready to continue on life's path with a brand-new set of luggage—you go, girl! Keep on keeping on—you're doing just fine.

Sis, I have to be perfectly honest with you. When you decide to empty out all the bad memories of the past and take an honest look at your life experiences, it hurts like hell! But honey, once you've passed through the fire and have overcome the pain (and you will), you become a spanking-new creature and an empowered and dynamic woman of color. You deserve to be the best that you can be in this lifetime. And you're not alone, because I'm walking with you through the process. You go, sis—keep on reading.

BEGIN WITH THE GREATEST LOVE OF ALL

Of all the relationships, the most important one you will ever have is with yourself. You spend more time with yourself than with anyone else, no matter how close you and someone else may become. But how many people actually take time to get acquainted with their own selves? Not many women listen to, speak with, or even like themselves. That's why we subconsciously (and many times consciously) allow others to run our self-value system.

Sis, you spend most of the day conversing with others. Why not put some time aside to influence your own mind? Start pumping some positive affirmations into your own thoughts. We are constantly being bombarded with reminders not to be selfish, but goodness gracious—we must not be selfless either.

RESOLVE AND DISSOLVE UNHEALTHY CHOICES

Here's a sister who decided to open her awareness to her own self, after experiencing too much bitter pain from letting past relationships define her:

> Dear Dr. Cornish,
>
> Thank you for loving sisters enough to write the book *10 Bad Choices That Ruin Black Women's Lives*. This book just reinforced what I didn't want to believe about me, always making bad choices in relationships, or should I call them "ships" because I always wreck. But now that I think about it, I am glad that (1) I am not the only woman that has this history, (2) with some hard, hard work, I can turn part of my life around, (3) that I am not crazy, just have a type of sickness.

I agree and thank you for the statement "In order to get ahead in life," for me in all areas, "we need to go back into our past and dig deep and uncover the patterns that we learned as a child." At forty-four years of age, it is definitely painfully hard to change the self-defeating behaviors that you labeled "self-hatred." This behavior has kept me allowing myself to be abused, used, and disrespected, all in the name of love or wanting to be loved.

The hardest area for me is to be aware of self-defeating behaviors and still act against them. It seems comfortable and familiar the old ways, and knowing that I am being a volunteer and not a victim is even more painful. I think I cry more with this new awareness. It is like an addiction that leaves me empty, broken, drained, and hopeless. My thoughts even seem like they are against me; [sic] saying, "why even try, you will always be the same, no one will truly love me, I'm getting too old to put new behaviors in effect."

It is beautiful black women like you who help women like me have "hope" that we can turn this cycle around. I want to change. I do not like being unfulfilled, getting a crumb and wanting it to be a loaf of bread. You talked about fear; I do believe I must have stronger fears than others in letting go of old behaviors.

I have made some changes in the past four and a half years, but not enough to where I am comfortable and confident about myself. I have been doing the internal work on myself through all types of self-help books, and the support of healthy women in my life, yet I have not come to the point of high self-esteem where I can stop my pain.

Although I've been told I have come a long way from "thinking" abuse was love and that I am supposed to compromise myself and my beliefs to be loved, I tire of it all. I have been in many therapists' chairs, still affirm myself, and definitely pray a whole lot. I just want some relief from the harm I cause myself at the hands of others.

Dr. Cornish, my question to you is: When does a permanent change come? Is there really an answer to that question?

I do look forward to one day meeting you, going to one of your seminars, or just even receiving a response from you. I just want to thank you once again for your truth, your mother's story, your aunt's story, and for just being another gift in my life, by way of God on my journey of change and growth.

Sincerely grateful,
Jasmine

YOU'VE GOT TO LOOK INWARD BEFORE YOU CAN MOVE ONWARD

My dear Jasmine,

Sis, I'm so proud of you for not giving up or giving in. You are on a powerful healing path. With every great change there are a lot of tears—it's the cleansing out and the washing away of the old habits to make room for the new choices. You are going through the "face it, erase it, replace it" process.

You did the difficult part by first *facing* that you have a situation that makes you miserable—now you are going through the challenging and very difficult stage of *erasing* the bad choices. It's powerful and confusing. The anger you feel is good. It is good because you are *now* realizing that you are valuable and wish you had not allowed yourself to be treated that unjustly in the past. What you are doing is taking back your power to run your own life.

Sis, you're going through a personal empowerment. Allow me to help you to process and release the anger with this positive affirmation: "I am guided and protected in every way by Divine powers. I am lovable, I am loving, and I am loved. God loves me, and *I deserve a good life.*"

Repeat this morning, noon, and night until it becomes a part of your very center—believe it with all your heart, and release your past mistakes. Forgive yourself. Say, "I've made some bad choices—so what? I'm ready to move to another level in life. I forgive *me,* and I forgive all others. I am now free to enjoy some good choices."

When you begin to feel a strange but comforting peace inside (and you will, I promise), then you are in the *replacing* stage. You are no longer the caterpillar crawling around in its cocoon, waiting for a change. You've now become the butterfly ready to spread her wings and experience new joy.

The joy comes and stays by realizing you are a human temple made up of a mind, body, and spirit. Sis, nurture your temple by getting in touch with your spiritual Creator. Read Saint Matthew 6 and 7 in the Bible. Take it one day at a time, and you'll see what good and permanent changes take place in your life.

Please keep in touch and let me know how you are doing.

SET THE TONE AT THE OUTSET OF ALL RELATIONSHIPS

Plenty of sisters have a lot of self-mending to do because of the wear and tear of being involved with commitment-phobic men. One of the most common questions I'm asked on my lecture circuit and seminar tours is "Can a man be satisfied with one woman?" The answer is yes. If he's mentally steady, he can; if he is emotionally unstable or commitment-phobic, he cannot.

It also depends on what the man is looking for in a woman. If he keeps straying, basically he's dissatisfied with something. Most men who have a lot of women are confused, but they won't tell you so. Multiple partners can serve as a way for them to escape from dealing with their insecurities. But some men simply enjoy sampling many women—partly because so many women make it easy for them. Women are the ones who actually dictate (not initiate) sexual situations with men. If a man makes an advance to a woman, and she refuses, he has to back off. Generally, men tend to be loose. A fantasy can catch them off guard in a split second;

and when they are caught off guard, they do not think before they act.

This is by no means meant to condone the behavior of the men, but if women wouldn't give sex so readily, men wouldn't be so loose. They would have no choice but to regain respect for women.

Women are prone to getting entangled in bitter unions because they've been falsely led to believe that there is a shortage of "good" men in today's society. So they've placed men on pedestals, cherishing them as prized treasures, no matter how badly the men treat them.

For instance, a man will tell a woman to have patience and give him a "little more time" to make up his mind, either about marrying her or about giving up seeing another woman. The "little more time" slips into weeks, then months, and then years; and still he sings the same song, and she still listens to the same lyrics.

If women would just realize that they are being used in these situations, and let the men know that they value themselves highly by telling the men exactly what they want from the relationship, they would be amazed how things would turn around for them.

I received this letter from a sister who decided to avoid the bitter and save herself for the better deal:

Dear Dr. Cornish,

I would like to thank you and your clients for *10 Bad Choices That Ruin Black Women's Lives*. I learned about your book through *Essence* and a coworker. They highly recommended it. I got the book and could not put it down until I completed it. I had decisions and revelations while reading it.

Prior to reading your book, a married black man expressed his feelings toward me. I was truly taken because I never experienced a married man interested in me. [For] months we had decent conversations because he was one of the few black men I could speak with, but I always sensed there was a greater interest.

He has shared his marital concerns with me. He is in the process of getting a divorce. In addition, he wants to spend time with me. I informed him I would give it some thought. The first chapter I read in your book was "Loving the Married Bachelor." I said, "I can't do it." I wouldn't want to be a part of ruining a marriage. I do like him because of our conversations, but I refused to be disrespectful. I know the effects of the "bad choices" I've made—they keep dysfunctional relationships.

I still cry in regard to them [bad choices], but I view the positive perspective. I am also dealing with the aftermath of being a survivor of incest. It's a challenge. I am learning to take care of me first. *10 Bad Choices That Ruin Black Women's Lives* is a great healing tool.

Halle

I contacted this sister and congratulated her for being so decent and for refusing to get entangled with this man and his promises of divorce. What a phenomenal woman—she has gone through so much, especially confronting her past experience of incest. You hang in there sis, and keep on the healing path. May God continue to give you clarity and blessing.

YOU DESERVE TO BE HEALED FROM THE PAIN OF THE PAST

Last November I was the guest speaker at a sisters' empowerment seminar in Manhattan. I was both hurt and surprised to learn about the enormous number of my precious sisters who have been molested, abused, or raped by an uncle or a cousin. When six women in the auditorium volunteered that they had been molested by their very own natural fathers at an early age, I got such a sharp pain in the pit of my stomach, it was as if someone had reached into my solar plexus and snatched out my internal organs. I had to ask for a few moments of silence, so that I could lift my spirit in prayer to God to ask Him to replenish my energy and guide me in helping my sisters to heal and empty out these painful memories.

A couple of the women were engaged to be married and admitted they were unable to fully trust their mates because of what they had gone through with their natural fathers. (Actually those creatures were only the sperm donors who helped to conceive them, because a true father would never harm his little girl like this.) A few of the other women shared that they became lesbians because of the bitter ordeal they underwent. I led them into prayer and an exercise "Nurturing the Interior Child," which I'll detail for you in "Good Choice #9: Rewriting Your Life's Script."

I had to make them realize the same thing I'm now sharing with you, sis: If you've been violated in any way, *it was not your fault. It was not your fault.* Someone unfairly took advantage of you, and the adult who was supposed to protect you failed. It wasn't you who failed. Please drop all forms of guilt. The exercises in "Good Choice #9" will help you to remove anger, fear, guilt, despondency, and frustration. You deserve to live a happy and loving life *now.*

I was able to help the sisters who were engaged to start building trustworthy relationships with their mates. I must openly share this with you just as I stated in the seminar: If you've decided to become a lesbian because of bad experiences with men, I don't agree with it, but it's not my place to judge you. That's a personal decision between you and God. But trying to escape from one sex to the other is not the solution. The real solution is to clear away the bitter experiences to make room for a higher form of love.

"LOOK BEFORE YOU LEAP"

Last December I received this letter. This young sister's dilemma moved me so much that I have to share her revelation with you:

Dear Dr. Cornish,

My name is Raquel, and I'm twenty years old. I just finished reading your book *10 Bad Choices That Ruin Black Women's*

Lives. I really enjoyed this book, but I have a slightly different situation, and I was hoping you could give me some advice.

I feel I should briefly describe my situation before I tell you the whole story. It involves me and another woman. Now this is the first woman I have ever dated. I do not consider myself lesbian or bisexual, and I don't feel as if I was experimenting. But since being with this one woman, I have not dated a man. When I think of dating, I'm more interested in women now, although I have yet to date another one. At the beginning of this year, I met a woman (Vanessa) at my workplace. Vanessa and I became friends, and shortly after we met, I found out she was not only a lesbian but she was (is) also married. She claimed she was "separated" and that she and her wife (Jackie, twenty-four) lived very separate lives. I was three months pregnant at the time. Vanessa began coming with me to all my prenatal care appointments, and she would frequently pick me up and drop me off from work when our schedules were similar.

I am a high school graduate and plan to attend college next fall. Vanessa is twenty-six and will be graduating from a Christian university in Ohio next year. As Vanessa and I began spending more and more time together, I began to develop feelings for her. We would often spend the night at each other's houses and sleep in the same bed. I was always afraid that one day Vanessa would leave me and go back to Jackie. The reason they were not together was because Vanessa had cheated on Jackie. They had been married for seven years. They haven't made love in almost two years.

As time passed, I started falling in love with Vanessa. Her wife is a flight attendant, and she worked every weekend. So I used to spend the night often. I would sleep on Vanessa's side of the bed, and she would sleep on Jackie's side.

My mother never liked the fact that Vanessa was gay, but she found out we were involved. My mother told me I couldn't be friends with Vanessa anymore, and if I chose to do so, I had to leave her house. So I ended up moving out of my mom's house and into Vanessa's, with her wife and her wife's family.

By this time I had met Jackie on two other occasions. My son was almost four weeks old by the time I moved in with Vanessa. Vanessa always told me that I could never give her what she wanted or what she needed. She constantly told me I was a child and she was an adult. But she continued to have a relationship with me. Vanessa always told me that she loved me but she was not "in love" with me. At the time I didn't know there was a difference. I'm not even sure I do now. I just know that what I was feeling was magical, but it was real and so intense. It still is. It's like nothing I've ever felt. I always felt like I was on "cloud nine" whenever we were together.

PUT YOUR HEAD BEFORE YOUR HEART

Once I moved in with Vanessa, everything changed. She was never there when I needed her. I cried almost every night, and she never knew. I felt like she was trying to hide her feelings for me from her wife. Before I moved in, she kept saying she wanted to be a part of my life forever, and she wanted to raise my son with me. I always believed everything she ever told me. (Yeah, I know I'm very naïve.) I just hoped they'd divorce so that Vanessa and I could be together. I wanted us to be a family.

Now Vanessa claims they're not as "separated" as they used to be. I had a conversation with Jackie, and I asked her how she felt about me and Vanessa being together, and she said she didn't care! She said she doesn't want to be with Vanessa because she cheated on her in the past and she's still not over that. But Vanessa had decided that she was going to wait for her wife.

My son is now four months old. Vanessa has already taken him to see her family. I have known her for ten months, and she has not introduced me to *one* person in her family. She tells her family that she got my son from a friend and that she's going to keep him. Only now she's decided to raise my son by herself. (Well, actually with her wife, even though she denies it.) She wants me to give up complete custody of my son. She wants to take him away from me. She says if I choose to raise him, I'll be doing it by myself and out of her house. I have agreed to give up custody because I feel I am not emotionally, mentally, or financially stable or able to take care of my baby on my own. I truly resent her for taking him away from me. Not only does she want to take my son away from me, she is taking him away for Christmas. She said she and her wife are taking my son to Denver to spend it with Vanessa's family. Thanksgiving they spent in Kansas. I hate her for taking my son away from me, but I still love her.

I depend on her emotionally, and I feel that is why I hurt all the time. I feel so alone, confused, and scared. I don't even want to live anymore. I cry almost every night. I've cried so much, I *can't* even cry myself to sleep. I feel like I have no reason to live. Without Vanessa or my son, I have nothing left. My mother doesn't even want me. She's practically disowned me twice. I haven't achieved anything worth living for except my son, and he's being taken away from me. I feel so empty and alone without them. Dr. Cornish, how can I let go and move on? I love her so much. My heart has been ripped to shreds. I don't think I can handle any more pain. I am dying on the inside. The pain is so unbearable. I can't bear it any longer. Please help me! I'm so alone and scared. I don't have anyone to turn to. Vanessa has been my rock for the past year. After I met her, I basically turned everyone else out. I am such a fool. A stupid naïve fool, but I am in so much pain. I really wish I was dead. Please help me. I'm at my wit's end!

Thank you for your time and consideration,

Raquel

GET RID OF ROTTEN LOVE

My dearest little sister,

You have been through so much and at such a young age. I promise you'll get beyond this, but you must be willing to take the advice I'm about to give you. Your letter troubled me so much that I had to get to it right away.

Sis, I never do anything without first praying to God to take the right step. . . . I prayed for you and this is what was revealed to me:

Raquel, you've been tricked by Vanessa (and Jackie). It's a wicked game to get your baby. From the very beginning it has all been a lie. Vanessa first saw you at work *pregnant*—she found out everything about you—got you to trust her, to "love" her. From the beginning, she assumed the parental role, went to prenatal classes with you. She tricked you into thinking it was because she cared about you, but it was *really* your unborn baby she was after. She and "her wife" can never have one of their own through their union, so they used you. (If it weren't you, it would have been some other unsuspecting young woman.) My God, Vanessa is wicked!

She is a mastermind manipulator like the devil himself. She has toyed with your emotions—gotten you so mesmerized and "feeling good" that you thought (or think) that you love her. Sis, you believed it was love *because of the way she made you feel about yourself.* In reality, she did a bait-and-switch number on you. The moment the trickster reeled you in and was sure she got what she wanted (your baby), she switched.

She is a liar, a cheat, and a user. Look beyond the surface— she has an ugly and corrupt spirit. She lied to you, Raquel. They (both her and Jackie) are after your baby—nothing more. Do not let these two culprits take your child away from you, not even for Christmas. You can see their true motive now by the way they are treating you—like an outsider.

This is what you have to do to save your and your baby's lives now: *Get out of that house immediately!* Don't look back. You cannot handle those two deceitful and demonic energies on your own. Vanessa (and Jackie) will tell you all kinds of "sweet nothings" (more lies), to rope you back in, until they're sure you can never take your son away from them. Then once they're sure, they'll throw you away again. Raquel, trust me with this—go and apologize to your mother. Tell her you're sorry and you *have* to come home for Christmas. Tell her you need her help to get your baby back. (Tell your mother everything.) If she refuses to help you in the beginning (because she's hurt or angry), please give her my number. We have to get you out of Vanessa's web now!

UNLOAD BEFORE YOU EXPLODE

First, do *not* let Vanessa know that you are taking your baby and leaving—*just do it.* Do not sign any papers giving your baby to them. And even if you have signed, it doesn't matter right now—you have to get that innocent beautiful little boy out of that lying, cheating, and corrupt household.

Raquel, you got caught up in a web of lies. Sis, you said you felt on "cloud nine" because it was a "new and exciting" experience for you. It was a "high" just like certain drugs are, but it's no good for you. It's unnatural (and confusing). That's why Vanessa and Jackie can never produce a natural child (a gift from God) out of their union—and they used you to get your child to complete their cheating "family."

Raquel, God loves you. We have a loving God who does not want you to be harmed or used in any way. Get a Bible right now and read these passages: Exodus 19:5 and Deuteronomy 30. Read these and believe that God is talking to you directly. To know that you are never alone, read these chapters in the New Testament: John 14, 15, 16, and 17.

Sis, God gives all of us a Holy Comforter (a personal guardian angel), but we have to pray and believe to receive assistance. Don't let Vanessa and her lying lifestyle block your greater blessings. Even though it may have felt physically "good" to you, look how emotionally, mentally, and spiritually "bad" you feel right now. Is it worth it?

Vanessa is destroying your life—she will do anything to get your baby from you. You are not important to her—you were the birth machine for a baby in her eyes.

Get out of her hold now! Take your *self* and your baby back from that lying wretch. *You can!* I promise. Call on God, and get your mother or a friend to help you. Keep repeating: "I am guided and protected by Divine powers of God." Memorize Luke 10:19: "Behold, I give you power to tread on serpents and scorpions, and over all the power of the enemy: and nothing shall by any means hurt you."

Please call me and let me know you and your baby are in your mother's home for Christmas.

I cannot explain the joy I felt when Raquel called me just before New Year's Day to share this:

Dr. Cornish, I just want to thank you for helping me. I didn't get out of Vanessa's house exactly on Christmas, but my son and I are out now. I'm not at my mother's house either, but I'm staying with a friend until I get my own apartment. My son is with his natural father until I get myself together. Thank you for helping me so much.

Amen, for getting rid of the old and starting anew!

Speaking of making new and good choices, it's time to avoid flimsy surface flings and choose a compatible partner on a higher spiritual level of intimacy. Let me take a moment to emphasize that there is a wide selection of good, decent, straight, single men who are looking for meaningful relationships. I hear from them through letters, e-mail, and my relationship seminars. Let's look at how to meet and relate to a stable and dependable mate:

ARE YOU READY FOR THE REAL THING, SIS?

William July II, best-selling author of *Brothers, Lust and Love,* teamed up with me to share some healthy, useful, and effective tips on creating compatible, long-lasting relationships with the opposite sex. Here are the key points of our dialogue, excerpted from my "Can We Talk Openly?" column in *Belle*:

GIVE YOURSELF PERMISSION TO BE LOVED

DR. GRACE: In life we come sandwiched between two pieces of paper—a *birth certificate* when we enter and a *death certificate* when we move on. The time in between is a beautiful gift from God. It's your birthright, so enjoy your journey. Don't waste precious time being angry at yourself, at men or at the world. We all do some foolish things at times, men and women alike. But you have a choice—to be as happy or as miserable as you wish, today. Somewhere along your path, someone may have hurt you—and you probably haven't liked yourself much since then. You've probably belittled yourself, cramped your own abilities, or allowed people to walk over you. You must stop hiding behind the pain.

Sis, realize that you're a beautiful human being who deserves to be loved by a loving person. But you must start by loving yourself first. Take a relaxing bubble bath, put on a pretty dress and some beautiful lipstick. Give the world a smile, and let people see just how lovely you are. William, what do you think?

WILLIAM: Life is about your relationship with yourself. God gave you a purpose to fulfill—and it's more than just being in a relationship. Women tell me stories of how they're holding on for dear life to some man who treats them worse than I'd treat my dog. They ask me why he's behaving the way he does. I ask them why they're staying with him. These women are taking terrible treatment because they're incomplete. If you're not complete, then you shouldn't be in a relationship. Incomplete women choose incomplete men. And two half-people equal one whole mess.

KNOW WHEN TO LET GO

DR. GRACE: I cannot emphasize this enough. One of the major reasons sisters have such difficulty in relationships is because we often bypass the nice, decent, sensitive men for the smooth-talking, incompatible users. If we turn on the tap and expect to get hot water—and hot water flows—then it's all right. But if cold water comes out, then something is wrong. Instead of looking into it, we rationalize that the water will eventually become warm—but it never does. Then, when the relationship goes wrong, we're horrified. All along we intuitively knew it was wrong, but we were afraid of letting go. Letting go is probably one of the hardest things to do in life, but even harder is the hurt you'll experience from an ill-fated union. You're too important for a mismatched mate.

WILLIAM: Have you heard the broken record: *Where are all the good men?* Sisters, what is a good man? Do you think a good man is about money, prestige, a perfect body, a certain education, or even the act of sex? Those are all temporary things that ride on the surface. When you're giving yourself in love, get hooked on the man for who he is *inside.* That's all you're really getting. Good men are all around you. The question is, can you see them?

BE READY FOR THE REAL THING

DR. GRACE: That's an excellent question. There are a lot of good men—but there are a lot of rotten ones who tarnish the reputation of decent black men and toy with the emotions of decent black women. They are the unconscionable Casanovas who unfairly judge sisters by superficial standards like hair, skin complexion, weight, status, and material possessions. I admonish sisters to avoid the "deadweight date" and choose and embrace the "heavyweight mate."

If you're looking for a Mr. Right, you have to become a Ms. Right. Compatible love is kindness, respect, and appreciation shown to each other. It doesn't come overnight. It has to be built. It involves consideration for each other's feelings (passing love's difficult test) and overcoming selfishness, false pride, and unforgivingness. There must be a healthy balance between the minds, bodies, and spirits of both partners.

WILLIAM: Ultimately, you must seek out a person with a strong character with whom you can match values. Notice I didn't say anything about income, job, body, skin shade, ethnicity, or any of the other superficial things. Your soul mate may be very different from you in surface appearance, profession, or income. But long-term relationships are the result of significant matches of values and harmony of spirit—not action under the sheet, money, or physical characteristics.

TAKE THE COMPATIBILITY TEST

DR. GRACE: Many people falsely believe that opposites attract. Opposites may create initial curiosity, but eventually they repel each other. Don't be misled by initial curiosity. Instead, select companions who think along the same lines as you, who support your ideas, ideals, and goals. Without similar ground, the relationship may last for a while, but eventually it will fail. We'd save ourselves from a lot of harmful situations if we'd get to know people well before embracing them into our hearts. Here's my menu for detecting an ideal mate:

A. Does his presence enrich my life in any way?
B. Is he looking out for my best interest?
C. Does he like me for the individual that I am (and not what he wants me to be)?

If you've answered yes to all three, there's an excellent chance you've found your "heavyweight mate." But be honest and analyze yourself on your mate's behalf too. If you've answered no to any of the above, the relationship needs some alteration. Always place a first-class value on yourself. Accepting an incompatible relationship is like taking a beautiful couture gown to be worked on by a five-and-dime tailor. You're too valuable to settle for a five-and-dime-minded mate.

WILLIAM: Amen to that. The most important thing in determining compatibility is first knowing yourself enough spiritually to know what you want from life. That knowledge will lead you to a peace that will put you in the right relationship, or at least give you the intuition and strength to avoid the wrong ones. Throw away any relationship rulebooks that claim to have a formula for love. God has already given you the key.

BYPASS THE BITTER AND GO FOR THE BETTER LOVING

Relationships are complicated because they involve two individual, separate minds. Success in a relationship depends on both people. We are no longer in our own individual world—we've merged with another human being and a new world; a new experience now exists. So depending on the mindset of both people involved, the relationship can be beautiful, caring and loving, or it can end up becoming destructive, harmful, and ugly. We are never the same during or after any relationship. We begin by forming our relationships, then along the way our relationships form us. At the outset, only our exteriors meet. We reserve our interiors from each other. Then when we progress, we become deeper, closer, and more intimate, and our interiors start to merge.

You've Got to Have Positive Reaction to a Chemical Attraction

Before entering a relationship, make sure you feel contented with yourself first, then bond together with someone who's at peace with himself. When two interiors blend, there is a new creation. It's like you're hydrogen and he's oxygen. Hydrogen and oxygen are each useful separately. But when they come together in combination, they form a new substance—water. On your own, you can have healthy self-love, but you will thirst for true romantic love. It is the union, the water, that brings forth deep love to quench the thirst in many lives.

When two exteriors come together, it is only an acquaintance. We've not reached deep within. We have merely touched at the boundaries. To reach to someone's interior, we must first be able to reach our own. That alone is a challenge.

If we really want to meet a man at his interior, we have to allow him to meet us at ours as well. This scares a lot of women because we have to become completely open, vulnerable, and exposed. But you must do this only if the man is mentally mature and spiritually receptive. It is very risky to expose ourselves to others because we don't know how they will treat us; so fear steps in—and with fear, unconditional love is impossible.

When we experience unconditional love, our individual barriers disappear. We become so compassionate and consumed with each other's souls that our surfaces become almost invisible. We venture deep within to each other's interiors. The relationship then becomes more meaningful, more spiritual, deeper. There are no struggles. All boundaries are removed. We simply blend together.

TRANSFORMING SCARS INTO STARS

Here's a sister who successfully took a leap of faith with compatible love:

Dear Dr. Cornish,

I was so happy to read *10 Bad Choices That Ruin Black Women's Lives*. I have to write you to give you my update. I'm Sonya. You shared my story at the beginning of "Bad Choice #4: Exchanging 'Sexual Dealings' for Loving Feelings." When I look back at myself on those pages, I can't believe how much I was starving for love. I've grown so much since then. I've got some good news for you. I'm presently engaged in a monogamous relationship. You had a lot to do with this. Let me tell you what happened.

Remember when you advised me over two years ago to "always remember three words: affection before erection"? It always stuck in my mind. When I didn't hear from Calvin after the last time we were together sexually, it hurt too much, and I felt like a flame on a candle that was about to flicker out.

I cried a lot and was disappointed. I realized that I really loved him and that I'd probably blown it because I slept with him so quickly. I only slept with him so soon because I wanted him to love me. Boy, did I go about it the wrong way. Anyway, I remember you said, "For any relationship to stand the test of time, you have to really *like* each other as friends, instead of loving each other's possessions."

You were so right, because even though I believed that I loved Calvin, I really didn't know him as a friend. (And he surely didn't know me either, except sexually.) I wanted us to get to know and grow to like each other. So I called him again—but this time, not to offer him sex. I called just to see how his day and life had been going. He was very pleasant (as always). I ended the conversation first, and he said he'd "call me soon." Two, three, four weeks passed, and no call from him. This time I didn't get upset because my goal was to become his friend. So I called again, light and warm greetings. This went on for over six months. I did all the calling, but he was always happy to talk with me, sometimes for over an hour.

As we talked more and more, we began to have more meaningful conversations. He began to open up to me and share some of his family background, goals, dreams, and past relationships. I found out that he was hurt in the past and wasn't ready to get into a long-term relationship. Whew! I realized I had another chance if I would continue to grow in friendship with him.

Once during our conversation, he hinted that he "missed me" (sexually). I told him the truth, that I felt ashamed for giving my body to him so quickly in the past, that I had been really hurt when he left, and when he didn't call, I felt cheap. Dr. Cornish, I can't tell you how that turned him around. He didn't say it in words but by his actions. I could tell that he was relieved that I didn't "make it a habit to sleep around." He started calling me to see how my day was going. He took me out on dates and never initiated sex. I had grown to really *like* him and could tell that he really liked me too.

IF SOMETHING IS TRULY YOURS, IT CAN NEVER BE TAKEN AWAY FROM YOU

Just as we were growing closer, he had a new and better job offer in another state. He accepted and would relocate in three months. I was happy for him but sad for me. I couldn't stop thinking about him. I kept praying to God that if this man was for me, to please let us be together, but if he wasn't, to please get him out of my system permanently. Well, I just couldn't stop thinking about him. I even questioned myself if I was obsessed with him, but I wasn't. I realized I simply loved him.

He took me out to dinner one evening, and I sort of hinted to him that I wanted a real relationship with him. He said he was interested, but he couldn't give me that because his entire life was about to change and he'd be relocating shortly. My heart sank.

The next couple of weeks he didn't call to see me, but his presence was constantly in the center of my mind and heart. I really fell in love with him. I had to let him know. So I prayed, and prayed, and prayed some more. I decided to write him a letter and not hold anything back. Dr. Cornish, this was so hard to do. I had to leave myself completely open and not hide in any way. I kept wondering if he would think I was a desperate and foolish woman, or if he would laugh at me. But something inside said, *Go ahead and tell him the truth from your soul.* I cried through the entire letter, but I wrote eight pages declaring my love for him, why I felt that way, and how I could be a plus in his life. I can't really explain, but writing that special letter freed me so much. I made up my mind that I had to do it—this would be the catalyst that would bring us closer together or let me get over him once and for all.

I received neither a phone call nor a letter from him for an entire month. But I kept focused on my own life, and I prayed a lot. My heart leaped when I (finally) got a letter from him. It also sank when I read his words, "I was flattered, but surprised and shocked that you feel this way. I care about you, always have. But I'm not in love (that doesn't mean I couldn't be). You'll always have a place in my heart, but I have to concentrate on my new career. Please promise me that this won't affect our friendship and you'll keep in touch."

Dr. Cornish, it did hurt. I cried to God like a baby. But it was a relief that I had finally let him know how much I cared for him. I realized that I was filled with love, and if he didn't want to embrace it, then that was his decision. I decided to take care of me. So I gathered my courage and dignity and wrote him again. This time I shared a new side of myself but still remained truthful, "I'm sorry I 'shocked' you, but I had to tell you the truth. Of course this won't affect our friendship. How could I be upset because you don't like me as much as I love you? I was sad but not angry. As a matter of fact, I turned to God and found out the romantic take to 'weeping may endure for a night, but joy cometh in the morning.' And I'm experiencing such a peaceful feeling in my soul that I will always love you as a friend anyway. I wish you the best and you will always be in my prayers."

That was it. I decided to let go and let God. Two months later I received letters and e-mail from Calvin telling me how he missed me—my voice, my laughter, and my presence in his life. He came back to visit me; we had a heart-to-heart talk. We shared our fears and joys with each other. We realized we were ideal together. And we've been together ever since. Praise God; and thank God for using you, Dr. Cornish.

Sincerely,

Sonya

I called Sonya to personally congratulate her on making a good choice, and she generously gave me this analogy: "Another way to describe my past relationship is, I felt as if I were in a peaceful room, with soft lights, listening to soft music, and it's as if someone abruptly flung the door open and sent twenty screaming kids running through. Imagine what a shock that was to my system. Now I'm in the peaceful room with no disturbances. I truly believe I've found my soul mate. Thank you for being patient and guiding me through the process."

ARE YOU READY TO BE BLESSED?

What a blessing! Your blessing is waiting for you too, sis. Just make sure you're prepared for it when it comes. In blessed relationships you give of yourself, but you don't give up yourself. You both give your hearts, but you do not lose your hearts.

Admire each other, but do not become each other. Enjoy your bonding, but do not crowd each other's space. You are two separate people who join together to enjoy common interests, but you must allow each other room to express your own selves. You are able to enjoy your activities apart from each other, but you gladly return to your partner to share them.

To sum it up, in your togetherness there is always closeness, yet always room.

good choice #3

Making Money Work for You

Wisdom is a defense,
and money is a defense.
Ecclesiastes 7:12

There are many myths about money. Many people believe it can make all their dreams come true. They earnestly declare, "I want money, lots of it. If I had money, I could do anything I want to."

Then there are those who attach a peculiar kind of guilt to having too much money. They claim, "I just want to make a good living. Just enough to pay my bills and live comfortably. I don't want to be rich." They believe, "Money is the root of all evil."

Now, let's get realistic here. There is nothing intrinsically evil about the possession of money. The way you get it can be evil. How you spend it can be evil. But money, in and of itself, can do no harm. It is people themselves who abuse the value we place on money.

Money is wonderful. It provides you with options. It allows you to choose among a variety of schools, homes, and vacation spots. Everything from your wardrobe to your stock market investment to your social activities is controlled by the amount of money you possess. It also directly affects your ability to be helpful to others. A person who has $100,000 possesses twice the capacity to give to others as does the person who has $50,000.

THE MORE MONEY, THE MORE CHOICES

During a segment on *Good Day New York*, another guest and I were invited to discuss tipping etiquette for the holiday season. The first guest shared that in Manhattan apartment buildings, it is "proper" and "expected" for each tenant to give each doorman at least fifty dollars as a holiday bonus. (Some buildings have at least ten doormen, so that comes to five hundred dollars.) When you add this sum to the other service tips—cleaners, supers, maintenance men, postmen, and so on—and to gifts for your family, friends, coworkers, and acquaintances, it can add up to quite a lofty sum.

I replied that you ought to give holiday bonuses according to your salary. It is not practical for someone who earns fifty thousand dollars to give bonuses in the same amount as someone who earns a hundred thousand dollars, even though they may live in the same building. I added that it would be wise to follow the example used in church, where you tithe according to your salary. Therefore, for holiday bonuses, you tip according to your earnings.

The host thoroughly enjoyed and agreed with my view, but the other guest got a bit annoyed when I commented that if the average person followed all the holiday bonus tipping "expectations" in New York City, she would be broke and frustrated by New Year's and would have to make resolutions for getting out of debt.

The guest just didn't get it. She got upset and exclaimed, "Well, what about the holiday spirit of giving?"

I smiled and responded, "The spirit of giving is not being debated here. People should give joyously—but only what they can afford. If you can afford to give only $25 to each doorman based on your salary, then give only $25. For those who can afford to give $75 and choose to do so, that's great. But if we want to really get to the heart of giving, let's talk about the true spirit of the holiday, which is to bring joy to friends and strangers alike. Why don't we talk about bringing the spirit to the hundreds of homeless people we pass and ignore on the streets in New York City each day?"

USE GOOD SENSE WHEN DEALING WITH YOUR DOLLARS AND CENTS

One of the most common sources of frustration is lack of money. If we have only one dollar to spend, let's not spend it all today. Many of us spend all our money today and leave ourselves broke for tomorrow—which leaves us in a state of want and aggression.

Obsessive overspending and mismanagement of finances makes us anxious, depressed, and frustrated. We must learn and understand how to control emotionally impulsive spending and figure out how to live within our means. Let's not spend a dime when we only have a nickel at our disposal.

Money is a necessary asset. For a woman, there are three ways to get money. You can inherit it, marry it, or work for it. Any other means would be illegal or immoral.

Let's take a look at these three methods of getting money. If you're one of the minute group of women who have inherited a fortune, you should skip directly over this chapter and proceed to the next. If you're presently "hoping" to "someday" inherit a fortune, then I'll keep my fingers crossed for you. If you're "wishing" to do so, it's time to wake up and get real.

The same applies to marrying money. If you genuinely fall in love with a man who happens to be rich, I wholeheartedly extend my sincerest congratulations. But if you're planning to marry for money only, then I strongly urge you to read the example of Heather C. in "Bad Choice #2: No Money, No Honey" in *10 Bad Choices That Ruin Black Women's Lives*. Heather's mission in life was to either marry a multimillionaire or not get married at all. She spent over four years, and all of her life savings, pursuing a

NFL football player. When she finally got his attention, all she received from him was a one-night stand and a quick brush-off.

To reiterate, it is wonderful to be in love with a good man. If he happens to be wealthy, great. But to choose marriage with money as your first love is to court disaster. Money is power, but don't let it overpower you.

EMPTY POCKETS CANNOT SUPPLY YOUR NEEDS

In one of my seminars, "Self-Enhancing Secrets for Black Women," I used the phrase "money is power." Out of the entire group, one sister in her mid-thirties, Patrice, got upset that I attributed power to money. Our conversation went like this:

PATRICE: I disagree with you that money is power. I'm very spiritual. With God you don't need money.

DR. CORNISH: Sis, don't misinterpret my words. Money is power, but it is not the *source* of our power. God is the source of our power. And He knows that we need money to take care of our necessities and pay our bills. That's why he gave us thinking minds—to find creative and honest ways to make money.

PATRICE: I still don't agree with you, because I pray to God and I get what I need. It's not the money. I needed a car about three months ago, and I had no money. I prayed to God, and I got my car. My sister bought it for me through God.

DR. CORNISH: Exactly—through God, our Almighty source. But what did your sister use to buy the car for you?

PATRICE: Two thousand.

DR. CORNISH: Two thousand what?

PATRICE: Two thousand dollars.

DR. CORNISH: Now do you understand? It took money to buy the car. But it took God to provide a way for you to get the money. Your sister didn't use two thousand smiles, or two thousand stones. It was two thousand dollars—the money—that made purchase. When your bills pile up, your rent, car payments, phone, utility, and credit cards, you have to pay your creditors with money. Don't misunderstand, money is not a substitute for God, but it is a powerful gift from God for us to use wisely.

PATRICE: I think people put too much emphasis on money. All I need is God and my Bible, not money.

DR. CORNISH: Sis, I understand where you're coming from, but you're still missing the point. I certainly couldn't function without God. I love Him with all my heart, and He guides my every step. I use the Bible for the principles I live and teach by. You have got to read and interpret it properly before you jump to conclusions. It tells you right there in Ecclesiastes 10:19, "Money answereth all things."

THE ABILITY TO ENHANCE YOUR MONEYMAKING TALENT IS A GIFT FROM GOD

Although the other participants in the seminar got the message, Patrice was still struggling with her belief about the importance of money. Finally, I explained: "Jesus, the very Son of God, knew the importance of money. When he went to Capernaum, a bill collector came to one of his disciples to collect tax money from Jesus. 'Doesn't your Master pay tribute?' the tax man asked Peter. Jesus could have easily said, 'I'll let my Father God worry about that. Money is of no importance to me. I have other business to take care of while I'm on Earth.' But no, sis—the Master responded in Matthew 17:27, 'Let's not offend them. Go to the sea, and cast a hook, take up the first fish, open his mouth, and you will find the necessary money; take it and give it to them from me and you.'"

Patrice finally got the point when I concluded: "Because Jesus was so straightforward about God's work, the Pharisees hated him and plotted about how they could entangle and get rid of Him by His own words. In those days, like today, if you did not pay tribute (your taxes), you were thrown in jail. Since Jesus taught about God, the Spirit, and the heavenly kingdom (so holy), they assumed He would disregard all earthly laws. They thought they had Him cornered when they cunningly asked, 'Master, we know that you are true and teach the way of God, and are not intimidated by the opinion and rules of men. Tell us, so all can hear, do you think it's really right to pay taxes to Caesar or not?'

"Jesus saw right through their wickedness and said, 'Why tempt, me you hypocrites? Show me the money. Whose image and subscription are on it?' 'Caesar's,' they said.

"'Then render unto Caesar the things which are Caesar's; and unto God the things that are God's.' Can you imagine how tongue-tied they where when He responded with this? Glorify God in the spirit, sis, but pay that which you owe on earth. With money you have the power to pay for what you want and need."

A Wrong Career Is Hard to Bear

So let's discuss how to get money. The majority of women neither inherit nor marry money; they work for their daily bread.

Your career occupies a large part of your life. It is very important to choose one that you will enjoy. Too many people look back on their career choice and think, "I could have been." They are merely functioning in their careers and are not happy. Many lawyers want to be actors. Many actors want to be doctors. Many doctors want to be musicians. Many musicians want to be preachers. Many preachers want to be teachers—the list is endless.

Surveys show that eighty out of every hundred people hate the work they are doing. Imagine, only twenty out of every hundred actually enjoy their professions!

That's a lot of miserable people. Their creative energies are being wasted because they are not doing what they really want to do. Instead of achieving their maximum, they are functioning at their minimum.

One-third of their day is spent doing something they don't care for. This gives them a lot of practice at being miserable. Practicing anything continuously makes you an expert. By doing something that makes you miserable, you can become an expert at being miserable.

Living as we do in a society that encourages freedom of choice, you would expect more people to exercise their right to choose (or create) a career that gives them satisfaction. Instead, they are psychological prisoners, dwelling behind the mental bars of a wrongly selected career.

WITTY WOMEN WIN AT WORK

The few who are doing what they love are psychologically free. They move ahead. They set trends. They get to where they desire to go. These people enjoy the good life. They are leaders in their fields—movers and shakers in the truest sense.

Let me pause right here to ask you one question, sis: Which life would you rather have? If you're satisfied with your career as it is now, then this section is not for you. But if you want to be one of the empowered sisters who are looking to be happy and successful in their careers, read on.

I have spoken with thousands of people, both average and empowered. These two groups think differently. Average people's lives are routine. Their duties have become burdens. Their tasks feel heavy, like weights on their shoulders, pressing them down. It is stressful for them to make any effort, mentally or physically. They would rather spend their energies on a different career, but this work is their livelihood. They work to earn enough money to meet their needs. Their needs have to be met so they can continue to work to earn enough money to meet their needs—and so on. They are traveling in a circle, and they are miserable.

Those are the "I could have been" people. And remember, eighty out of every hundred people you know belong in this classification.

Now, let's take a look at the empowered group, to which you belong. These people are in love with their work. They get a deep sense of fulfillment from their performance. They are free of worry. They look forward to going to work every day. Many would continue to work even if they were not being paid for it.

This is the advantage of the empowered. They are in careers that they enjoy doing. They labor with love. Here you have two very different ways of thinking:

The Average: "I do this work because I need to do it."
The Empowered: "I do this work because I like to do it."

Six Excuses for a Bad Career Choice

Millions of people feel stuck in their present position. They use many excuses to rationalize their situation. The most common are:

1. "I want to change careers, but I'm being paid very well."
2. "I never wanted this profession, but this is what my parents wanted."
3. "I hate this job, but I'm too old to change now."
4. "I want to get a better job, but I'm not qualified."
5. "I would like to succeed, but people are always being unfair to me."
6. "I want a job I can enjoy, but I'm afraid of going on interviews."

Let's examine these more closely:

EXCUSE #1: "I WANT TO CHANGE CAREERS, BUT I'M
BEING PAID VERY WELL."

After graduating from college, Betty G. was hired as an assistant store manager for a chain of specialty clothing stores. By the time she left, she had worked her way up to the position of store buyer. Seven years ago, at the age of thirty-four, she was hired by another company, which promoted her several times. She is now vice president of operations. She works an average of sixty-five or seventy hours a week. She is very well paid. But she is unhappy in her job.

One Saturday, while attending a charity luncheon sponsored by a mutual associate of ours, Betty and I met, and our conversation eventually turned to the subject of her career. Her attitude suddenly changed from cheerful to grim.

Concerned, I asked, "What's the matter? Are you all right?"

She sighed, paused for a few seconds, then hesitatingly revealed, "You know, I have invested many years in reaching this position, and now that I'm here, I can't enjoy it. I strongly dislike my job."

"Why don't you do something else?" I asked

"That's easier said than done," she responded, as if she were disappointed with herself. "I've put a lot of time in this company. I have been trained for this profession. I've built my life around it. I am really tired of the long hours I have put in; I'm tired of being stressed out. I hardly have enough time to spend with my husband and children."

"Is it the type of work or the company you work for that you dislike?" I inquired.

"Both," she quickly responded. "I would actually like to start my own business. But I am being paid very well now. My husband makes much less than I do. We need the money to support our family. I don't know if I would be able to make this much money if I had my own business."

Trying to be encouraging, I asked, "If you compiled a list of the contacts you've made throughout the years, couldn't you use them as a base to set yourself up as a consultant? That way you could first test it out on a part-time basis and then build to full-time from there."

"Mmmm...yes—but my time is tightly rationed," she replied. "As it is now, I hardly have any to spare. Maybe sometime down the line I'll look into it. But right now I can't afford to take the gamble. At least I'm making good money."

Betty G. is doing a job she hates for the sake of the money. It is affecting her personal and social life as well as her business. She is unable to enjoy the money she is making because she is so unhappy. But she stays in her job because of the money—and around she goes on the financial treadmill.

EXCUSE #2: "I NEVER WANTED THIS PROFESSION, BUT THIS IS WHAT MY PARENTS WANTED."

Dr. Gwendolyn P. is a reputable dentist for a family-operated clinic. I've known her for over five years. Her patients are very loyal. Her interests are diverse. Although she is a very pleasant person, she always seems to have an unhappy look on her face.

One Wednesday afternoon, I visited her clinic. She has an extensive music collection in her office. Classical, country, reggae, jazz—everything. I was intrigued. "Dr. P., you have a whole variety of tapes here," I remarked.

Her face lit up as she responded, "That's my private escape. Music is my best friend. I appreciate all kinds. I have an even bigger collection at home. I listen to music constantly—while working, driving, even in the shower." She paused, then smiled. "It's funny—my husband teases me that I'm having an affair with my music collection. He says I spend more time listening to music than with him."

I was amazed at the change in her expression—once music was mentioned, she became animated. "Well, doc," I joked, "I guess it's safe to say you're swept away by music."

Her facial expression returned to its usual somber look. Regretfully, she explained, "While growing up, all I ever wanted was to become a musician. I wanted to create music—my music—for people to enjoy."

"Why didn't you pursue your dream?" I asked.

She sighed. "When I first presented the idea to my parents, my father became very annoyed. My mother was a bit more understanding, but she eventually sided with my father. Being from a wealthy black family, my parents expected their children to either be doctors or marry doctors.

"You see, my father was also a dentist. He had always dreamed of having a son to follow in his footsteps. But all four of their children were girls. As the firstborn, I became the substitute son. He was a good and loving father—I've always respected and admired him. But he was very set in his ways. It hurt him to know I wanted to be a musician instead of a dentist like himself.

When You Give Up Your Dreams, You Give Up Part of Yourself

"I remember quite vividly the day I decided to give up my hope of becoming a professional musician. I was sixteen, in my junior year in high school. It was time to submit applications to the colleges of my choice.

"I was sitting at the dinner table with my parents and sisters. I brought up the subject of pursuing music as my undergraduate major. I'll never forget the look on my father's face. He was both astonished and angry. For the first time in my life, he raised his voice at me. 'I thought this matter was already settled,' he said. 'You will be specializing in dentistry. Your mother and I have selected the three top institutions in the field for you to choose from. You know we love you. We want only the best for you. We have always been proud of you. Don't disappoint us now. I want you to join my practice and take over the clinic when I'm gone.' Then my father broke down. I had never seen him that way before.

"My mother pulled me aside and told me I was breaking my father's heart. She pleaded with me to do as he wanted. I felt guilty for causing my parents so much grief. I loved them and wanted them to be proud of me.

"Well"—she took a deep breath—"from that day on, dentistry became my specialization. And here I am. It pleased my father. He was so proud of me. I worked alongside of him right here in this office. He passed away seven years ago. I'm glad I was able to make him happy. But I wish he understood me. He stood in the way of my happiness. I have a wonderful husband and two lovely boys. My father was still alive when my first son was born. His wish was for my son to carry on the family practice. But I've decided to let my children choose for themselves.

"I've always felt as if something were missing in my life," she sorrowfully concluded. "I fill this void by listening to music—music composed by someone else."

Dr. Gwendolyn P. was railroaded into a profession she didn't choose. Most children wish to please their parents, and most parents mean well. But they should realize the damage they can cause by trying to remake their children in their own images.

Remember, your parents want you to succeed. They want you to be happy. Once they understand it is better for your mental well-being to pursue the work you desire, they will support your interest. Even if your parents do not approve, you should still follow your own desire.

EXCUSE #3: "I HATE THIS JOB, BUT I'M TOO OLD TO CHANGE NOW."

Cassie E. is a fifty-three-year-old cosmetics-counter manager in a major department store. She has been with the same cosmetics company for over seventeen years. She is divorced and has two grown children, a thirty-two-year-old son and a twenty-four-year-old daughter, both of whom still live at home.

While consulting with this company, I had the pleasure of

meeting Cassie. She is a very dynamic sister. When dealing with customers, she sparkled with delight. But while performing the other facets of her job—taking inventory, stocking merchandise, tallying daily sales figures—she was not at all enthusiastic.

One afternoon Cassie asked to speak with me. She confessed she wasn't pleased with her career. "I've always wanted to work in public relations," she explained. "I like working with people very much. But my husband never allowed me to work. He was strongly against the idea of having a wife with a career. So I never got the necessary training. After he divorced me, I had to go out and work. I took a job as a salesperson for this cosmetics line. I've been with the company since it was first formed.

"I am loyal to them. But I keep wishing I could work in public relations. The closest I'll ever get is dealing with customers. I'm sure it's not the same, but I have to make do.

Don't Give Up on Your Need to Succeed

"I come here every day just to earn my weekly paycheck," she continued sadly. "I have been here all these years. I'm tired of the same boring routine. I wish I'd followed my own mind when I was younger. I would have been doing what I really want to do." She was almost crying.

Trying to comfort her, I inquired, "Why don't you look into some adult education courses on public relations? You can take them in the evenings or on Saturdays."

"At my age?" she asked. "It's almost time for me to retire."

"You still have at least ten years before retirement," I replied. "This gives you an entire decade in which to do the work you really want."

"My opportunity came seventeen years ago," she grimly responded. "I should have taken it then. I can't go back in time."

"But you can go forward," I urged, trying to get her to see that she could change her life if she had faith. "You are alive and healthy. You can start following your interests right now."

"No, it's too close to my retirement," she answered. "I have only twelve more years to work. After that, I can rest. In the meantime, I'll just do my job."

Cassie is using the "I'm too old" excuse. It's very common—she has given up. She has cemented herself into an atmosphere she finds unrewarding. She has traded in twelve energetic, useful years of doing what she really wants for twelve years of waiting for her work life to end.

It isn't just people over fifty who use this excuse. Many women in their forties and even in their thirties and late twenties are convinced that they are "too old" to relinquish a career they dislike.

EXCUSE #4: "I WANT TO GET A BETTER JOB, BUT I HAVE TO WAIT UNTIL I'M PERFECTLY QUALIFIED."

One of the saddest examples I've ever seen of someone not using her potential to obtain a lucrative career is Marla W. She is an exceptionally brilliant sister with a superior analytical mind and extraordinary powers of concentration.

With such qualities, one would expect to see her profile in *Who's Who*. Unfortunately, it is not there. She is an unknown architect, working for an obscure firm.

The problem is that she tries to do everything perfectly. For example, she selects a company to present her ideas to. She begins to draft a proposal. She thoroughly researches the field. She works around the clock, sometimes on as little as four hours of sleep. Once she is finished, she'll decide the project is not as good as it could be. She'll then conduct more extensive research. She'll rewrite the proposal at least ten times. It never becomes perfect enough to present. Because of her addiction to perfection, she remains at the same professional level.

Her frequent excuse is "It's very competitive out there. I always have to be one step ahead of the rest. I need a little more time. I'm getting it together." She has been "getting it together" now for over thirteen years. Her compulsion to get ahead has caused her to remain behind.

Marla has tripped on life's career path. There is nothing wrong with falling, as long as you get up, brush off the dirt, and try again.

People who are always looking for the perfect way to do everything end up doing nothing. They are always waiting until "later." They rationalize, "Since I don't have enough experience, I will wait until later to apply for a better job," or "I'm not financially secure, so I'll get married later," or "I don't have the right type of furniture yet, so I'll invite my friends to my home at a later date."

But, like "tomorrow," "later" never comes. If you're waiting for the "perfect" time to do something, you'll be waiting for eternity. There is no time like the present. Start now. Ten percent of something is better than a hundred percent of nothing.

EXCUSE #5: "I WOULD LIKE TO SUCCEED, BUT PEOPLE ARE ALWAYS BEING UNFAIR TO ME."

Many people are full of excuses for not taking control of their own lives. How do we develop this dependence? There are two reasons. First, our parents may have neglected to teach us self-reliance. And second, we may have neglected to take responsibility for ourselves.

The story of thirty-seven-year-old Patricia, an "aspiring" actress, will bring this point home. She is the firstborn of three children. Her father, now sixty-eight, is a retired lawyer. Her mother, fifty-nine, is a housewife. Patricia has always been the apple of her parents' eyes. Her younger brother and sister have always been lost in her shadow.

As far as her parents were concerned, Patricia was always right. Whenever she received a low grade, her parents would say, "Don't worry. You're not to blame—you did your best. We'll have a word with your teacher." This applied to all areas of her life. At cheerleading tryouts, the captains were biased; in elections for school club president, the students were unfair. Patricia learned two things from this:

1. Other people didn't treat her fairly.
2. She could always rely on her parents to take her side.

When Patricia got married, the farewell from her parents was what you would expect: "You know we will always be here for you, just in case things don't work out the way you want them to."

Naturally, as in all marriages, some minor misunderstandings arose in Patricia's. But her parents were right there telling her, "You know, Pat, Steve isn't right for you. You're not responsible for his actions. It's unpleasant that he's not treating you the way we do."

They led Patricia to believe she was not to be blamed for this predicament. This pattern continued. Divorce followed. Back to her parents she went.

Meanwhile, Patricia had been turned down for numerous acting roles. At auditions, she believed, "the casting agents could not appreciate good talent." She finally got cast in an Off-Broadway play. During the third rehearsal, she was asked to leave. She felt it was because "the director wasn't creative enough to appreciate her style."

Patricia got her other jobs through her father's contacts. But she quickly lost them because "they were envious of Patricia, so they wouldn't keep her on," or "they were not treating Patricia fairly."

Patricia is still at home, depending on her parents to rescue her. Sis, people who take total responsibility for themselves and use no excuses obtain the best jobs and relationships and the most joy in life.

"I will always have my parents or my old job to fall back on." "I don't have to deal with the world." These excuses are the seeds of failure.

EXCUSE #6: "I WANT A JOB I CAN ENJOY, BUT I'M AFRAID OF GOING ON INTERVIEWS."

Wendy K. is an example of a sister whose fear prevents her from obtaining a rewarding career. She is thirty-two, from a black middle-class background, and has never worked.

A very bright and articulate person, she got married after completing only her first year of college, and she dropped out during her second year, eleven years ago. She recently returned to school and graduated with a bachelor's degree in marketing. She is very unhappy in her marriage, but because of financial insecurity, she is afraid to leave.

Fear dominates every area of Wendy's life. She has never lived on her own. She wants to move into her own apartment, but she has gotten used to the material comfort that even a bad marriage can give.

Wendy wants to get a job in marketing and schedules herself for four or five interviews weekly. But because of her fears, she will go to only one, if any.

This was one of our conversations about her career options:

WENDY: I'm ready to get a job now, but I hate going on interviews.

DR. CORNISH: Why?

WENDY: I feel I'm being judged by a stranger. I don't know if I'm what they are looking for. I don't like that feeling.

DR. CORNISH: It's natural to be a little apprehensive. You're meeting a stranger who has the authority to decide whether you will get something that's important to you.

WENDY: That's what makes me so nervous. I'm afraid they'll think I'm not good enough. And when I get nervous, I say the wrong things.

DR. CORNISH: If you're not offered the position, it doesn't mean you're not capable. There are many applicants for every position. Interviewers face quite a challenge, selecting just one candidate out of sometimes hundreds. Don't look at it as something personal. Just do your best.

Aquire the Desire to Move Ahead in Life

"That's just it," she responded. "My best is all I have to give. And it hurts me when it's rejected. All my life I've felt rejected. The only attention I received was when something went wrong and I got punished." She was bringing up past hurts. "I've lived with the fear of always having to mind what I said. I'd get reprimanded for reasons I didn't even understand. I was always picked on in my home. This still hurts me very much. Because my own parents treated me like this, I grew up believing everyone else would, too.

"To protect myself, I kept my true feelings inside—safe and away from the rest of the world. I know I'm fearful," she added. "I'm the first one to admit it. I'm fearful every time I leave my house. I'm fearful of going to new places, meeting new people— I'm afraid of going into the job market." She paused briefly, then added, "It won't be so bad after I get past the interview. But I just have to work my nerve up to do it."

After expressing her feelings so openly, she looked relieved. Yet her fear of interviews remained.

DR. CORNISH: You know, Wendy, I have to give you credit for being honest with yourself. You have brought your unhappy childhood experiences with you into adulthood. You have taken the responsibility to acknowledge your fear. This is the first step toward healing yourself. Before you can correct something, you have to first realize that it needs fixing. It will take a little while to mend everything. But start with your most immediate need. What's the first thing you'd like to accomplish?

WENDY: I'd like to get out of this marriage so I can live in peace and decide what I want to do with my life. I have to have money to move on. To get money, I need a job; to get a job, I have to be interviewed. [brief pause] I'll do it soon.

Visualize the Drive to Survive

"I want to try a visualization-affirmation approach, which I believe will solve your interview phobia," I stated. "Relax and close your eyes, and imagine yourself doing what I'm about to describe." When she was ready I began: "Picture yourself walking into a company for a job you really want. You're asked by the receptionist to submit your résumé. You are then asked to fill out an application. You hand her your completed application and sit down. She takes your papers a few doors down the hall, to be reviewed by Mr. Interviewer. While you are waiting, think of how comfortable you are. Tell yourself, 'I feel a little nervous, but it's only the excitement of being someplace new. This is nice; I like this place; I feel at home.' Familiarize yourself with the surroundings. Observe the chairs, the plants, and the paintings.

"The receptionist tells you, 'Mr. Interviewer will see you now.' While you are being escorted into his office, visualize Mr. Interviewer as a friend of yours. A companion with whom you feel relaxed—one to whom you can truly speak freely. You enter his office. You see Mr. Interviewer's friendly face. You greet each other. This friend offers you a seat. You feel at ease. You are both seated, having a pleasant conversation. This friend asks you questions about yourself. You delightedly answer. You relate all of your positive experiences and accomplishments pertaining to the job.

"You are very interested to learn more about this company. You enthusiastically ask some interesting questions. Your friend eagerly answers. You both have your inquiries satisfied. Upon leaving, you shake hands, smile, and tell your friend, 'I hope to be hearing from you again.' You confidently leave."

"It's not easy to see a stranger as my friend," Wendy declared, as she opened her eyes.

"You have to practice," I replied. "Just like everything else, it takes time. Try it at least once. From now on, think of interviewers as companions. The only way to overcome fear is to do the very thing you're afraid of. Deliberately force yourself to attend interviews, even for jobs you don't really want. Use them as rehearsals to gain experience. When you feel quite confident, go after the ones you really want."

"Don't Knock It Until You've Tried It"

The conversation ended with Wendy sounding very apprehensive. "I don't know, I'll try," she offered.

About two months later, I received a call from Wendy. She sounded very enthusiastic. To be honest, for the first few seconds, I didn't recognize her voice, she sounded so optimistic.

WENDY: Hi, doc, guess what?

DR. CORNISH: What?

WENDY: [*happily*] I'm not afraid anymore.

DR. CORNISH: Of interviews?

WENDY: Yes! Nor am I afraid of anything else!

DR. CORNISH: You sound wonderful. What happened?

"I've been thinking a lot about what you said about perceiving interviewers as my friends. I've been doing it, and it's working!" She continued joyously, "I've been practicing doing things I like—things I've been afraid to do. I used to feel so uncomfortable in my own skin, and now I feel at home. I realize it's going to take time and effort to completely change myself, but I've started.

"It feels good. The only way I can explain it is, I feel as if I've just bought a new pair of shoes. They squeeze a little because they're new. It'll take time to break them in. But the more I wear them, the more comfortable they'll feel."

Wendy has seen for herself that the way to conquer fear is to do what you are afraid of doing. Way to go, sis!

THE INVESTMENT BANKER WHO BECAME A FLORIST

Donna S. was thirty-nine and an investment banker for a large firm on Wall Street when she decided she wasn't getting the most from her career. Although she liked banking and had devoted over fifteen years to the field, she felt that something was missing from her professional life.

"I knew I was performing well," she explained. "I was being paid very well. But I had to push myself to get the work done. My heart wasn't in it. It began to affect my health. I would go home with headaches practically every day. Fridays were fine because it was the end of the work week. I looked forward to Saturdays. But on Sundays the migraines would start again because I had to be at work the next day.

"I had always known what I really wanted to do. But I kept it to myself. As a little girl, I had always loved the beauty and smell of flowers. I had promised myself that I would have my own flower shop when I grew up. About three years ago, I went to visit the Botanical Gardens in the Bronx for the first time. My long-suppressed dream of being a florist suddenly resurfaced.

"Every time I thought about leaving banking, I felt foolish. I had gone to college and to graduate school to prepare myself for this profession. I thought only a fool would give up fifteen years' experience and fifty-five thousand dollars' worth of schooling.

"The other problem was I was divorced, with two sons to support. I was afraid to take the chance. But one Saturday I worked up enough courage to ask my mother's advice about this. I told her I believed I'd made a big mistake in my choice of career.

"To my surprise, she was very supportive and very interested in my dreams. She asked me many questions. She said, 'Making a mistake is not bad, but doing nothing to correct it is.' She also told me she would be by my side through the transition from banking to my new profession."

Donna S. became a florist. She opened a flower boutique in Westchester County. I received a postcard from her two months ago. She wrote, "Dr. Grace, I was good in banking, but I'm even better with flowers. I'm opening another boutique in July. I'm doing well. Hope to see you soon."

Donna S. is one of the empowered sisters who prove that a person can do anything she wants, if she honestly makes the effort.

It Isn't Where One Is That Matters, but Where One Plans to Go

A young, bright-eyed sister came to see me after my workshop and asked if she could talk with me for a few minutes. She told me the discussed topic, "Self-Motivation Through Optimism," was very important to her.

Rebecca J., twenty-nine years old, had been through some difficult times, but she was now preparing herself for a better future. We spoke about the tremendous impact of a positive outlook. We discussed how important it is for people who are economically challenged to believe in themselves in order to improve their futures. She went on to say:

"I live in a small apartment in an underprivileged area. My rent is high. I have less than three hundred dollars in the bank, and I don't make much money at my job. But Dr. Grace, I refuse to be trapped in this standard of living. I am determined to get ahead and do well."

I was very impressed by this vibrant sister's outlook and asked her to continue.

"I'm making a map for my future," she delivered. "Every day I'm surrounded by people who complain—my friends, my neighbors, my coworkers. They continually go on about the bills, lack of money, and their hopes of winning the lottery. They are miserable with their surroundings because they see life only as it is today instead of planning for a brighter tomorrow."

She was speaking from deep within. After a short pause, she added, "I know where I want to be over the next couple of years. I see myself in a higher-paying job, as an executive. I will live in a better home. I will be able to vacation in foreign countries, and I will help my mother with my younger brother's and sister's upbringing. I'm taking the necessary steps to get there. I'm educating myself in business, through related courses and seminars. And the right doors have already started opening for me."

Rebecca J.'s outlook proves she is a successful thinker. This dynamic sister is on the fast track to fulfilling her dreams.

The Practical Moneymaking Secret

Sis, we've now come to a very critical stage on your path toward empowerment and peace of mind. You already know that a certain amount of financial security is necessary to free your mind from worry. Having enough money to live the way you deserve calms and soothes the mind.

Anyone who says she does not want money suffers from feelings of inadequacy. She is like the teenager who feels she can't make the cheerleading team or the honor roll, so she pretends she doesn't care about cheerleading or the honor roll.

Money is an object to be desired. What is undesirable is people who put money above everything else. These are usually people who have only small amounts of money. The reason: People who give money top priority seem to overlook the fact that money cannot grow without being properly nourished.

The nourishment is service. The empowered sisters who have put good work above money are happy in their careers. They are doing well because they are doing what they like.

The average person's reason for choosing her career is "I hear there's a lot of money to be made in this field." They end up choosing a career that they do not enjoy, and their performance becomes mediocre at best.

The truth is that money, a decent amount of it, can be made in every field. Many people say, "I'm going to be a lawyer because there is a lot of money in law," or, "I'm going into real estate because that's a big moneymaking area," or, "I want to get into such-and-such a career because I hear people make a lot of money in it."

Such thinking can trap you into selecting a field that may not suit you. But if money is your priority, you choose it anyway. This is a very costly mistake—costly for both your mental and your physical health.

Certainly there are many wealthy lawyers. But a lot of lawyers are also quite poor. And although real estate has its share of rich entrepreneurs, many are barely getting by. This holds true for doctors, preachers, models, and any other career group.

MONEY WILL GROW *WHEREVER* YOU PLANT GOOD SEEDS

Every career—even a field like teaching or social work, has its enterprising earners. Even if they don't work in traditional "big money" jobs quite a few of these people are financially well off.

Every career has "riches" in it. There are no "poor"-paying ones. Outstanding people can make money in all areas. The problem is, there are a lot of people in careers who really shouldn't be there. The secret to making money is to do what you really like, and the money will follow. When you labor with love, you do it with maximum effort, and people pay good money for good work.

There is no one particular career that will bring success. Success is available in all fields. It depends upon you and your priorities. If you place moneymaking at the top of your list of priorities, you will be unsuccessful. If you put purpose first, you'll be on your way toward true wealth.

The problems with this "money on top" attitude are exhibited by a young lady I worked with many years ago.

Mary T. was like a lot of people you know. She was always focusing on her *need to* make money instead of trying to find out *how to* make money. She spent most of her working hours going over her personal money problems.

She would complain, "This company is making millions. It's a big business. A lot of people are being paid large salaries, so I should be, too."

Many times Mary T. had been passed over for promotions and pay increases. One day she decided to demand a raise. Half an hour later, she returned angry, grumbling, "I'm so disgusted with this company. I asked the personnel manager for a raise. She had the nerve to ask me why I thought I deserved one.

"I gave her a lot of reasons. I told her I've been working here for almost a year. And everyone else was getting raises. And I needed the money more than most of them—I told her my bills were stacking up higher and that I always did whatever they wanted me to.

"All she said to me," Mary continued, "was that when my record showed I deserved a salary increase, I would get a salary increase. She acted as if I were begging for a handout. I would do a better job if they'd pay me better. I'm not burning myself out for this small amount of money."

You Must Use, Not Lose, Your God-given Talent

Mary is one who cannot see the *how* in moneymaking. She expects to be paid in advance for job performance, then she will deliver. But companies just don't function like that. You are given a salary increase for doing excellent work, not for promising to do so.

People do pay for good service. The executive who serves the company's best interests can expect to climb the corporate ladder. The salesperson who gives complete service gains large commissions. The waitress who gives the best service doesn't have to worry about good tips.

People are used to receiving only average service. Give them more than they expect, and they'll pay you handsomely for it. Even a simple thank-you and a pleasant smile go a long way. When you are in a profession you enjoy, doing it well will come naturally to you.

FIND YOUR FIT

Have you ever tried to fit a square peg into a round hole? What a frustrating endeavor! Have you noticed that people who are unhappy with their careers are mentally frustrated? Like most people, they work all their lives so they can have enough money to retire. But being stuck in a job or career they hate makes them stressed out and even physically sick. By the time they retire, they're so sick, they don't get to enjoy the money they've saved, because they have to use it to pay doctors' bills to cure them of the accumulated stress and aggravation.

Sis, for your own well-being, *make money work for you* by getting into a career or business that gives you satisfaction.

good choice #4

Turning Stumbling Blocks into Stepping-Stones

Behold I give unto you power to
tread on serpents and scorpions . . . and
nothing shall by any means hurt you.
Luke 10:19

Have you ever felt that you don't know whether you're going to make it, but you just know that you have to make it?

Sometimes the past catches up with you, the present looks dim, and the future is nowhere in sight. You feel like you don't know what your purpose or position is; you can't feel your way through the numbness. Your relationships have repeatedly gone bad; your home, job, and social environments have no flavor; you feel as if you're in suspended animation. You silently plead, "Lord, please give me a reason why I should go on." You clutch to the belief (or hope) that if only the right man, right job, or right diet would affix itself to you, it would remove all obstacles and jolt you back into "the land of the living."

You may even feel as if you've been sleepwalking through life, or bumping into concrete walls—merely existing and taking what has been dished out to you. You may have maxed out your credit cards or packed on the extra pounds, and you just don't know where to start. You agonize, "How can I get my life back on track," or, "How can I get my body back? Does it make sense to even try?" "Have I missed out? Am I too old—God, I need a rebirth!"

You may feel that you've tripped on life's path for the thousandth time, or tripped over your own feet, or somebody else's feet, or just been tripped by the fear of tripping. Whether you're in your twenties or your fifties, at this point of self-evaluation, you're wondering, "Where have all the years gone? My life is not going the way it's supposed to. What's going on?"

DON'T WAIT FOR TOMORROW TO START LIVING TODAY

Sis, we have come a long way.

We were first torn from the womb of our motherland and were brought to this country to be abused, mocked, and shunned. Then we were stripped of our dignity, pride, and self-respect and were forced to accept a new homeland. But—that was yesterday.

Today we have journeyed far beyond the chains of bondage, laws of segregation, and denial of education. We have become teachers, lawyers, and psychologists. By now we should realize that we are no longer helpless. But we still have a long way to go.

Every day millions of us complain about how miserable, helpless, and worried we feel. We are glad the past is over, yet we are not enjoying the present, and we are fearful of the unknown future. We spend our lives striving to "become someone": someone happy, someone wealthy, someone famous, or any "someone" other than the "one" we presently are.

We're always wishing for a better life, a different life, or a new life. We spend precious time yearning and hoping instead of embracing and enjoying. This is a tragic state because we only have one life, sandwiched by two pieces of paper: a birth certificate when we enter, and a death certificate when we pass on.

The span between these two documents is a sacred gift from God. It's a limited journey, to be sure, but even though we can't change that fact, we *can* change our outlook. Sis, we can create a new awareness to improve our lives and enjoy our special allotted time on the planet. We can erase our old thinking of fear, despondency, and loneliness, and we can replace it with new feelings of comfort, joy, and love.

An unhealthy disposition cannot supply us with an enjoyable life. We can't celebrate life if we're always asking, "When will I be happy?" or "Where's my slice of the pie?" Nor can we afford to postpone life: "I'll be happy *after* I become successful, famous, rich, married, thin, promoted" or any other *after* that we treasure. When we eventually accomplish our goal and still have not found happiness, we are puzzled.

Sis, like *tomorrow, after* never comes. The time to enjoy our lives is in the *here and now* of today, not the uncertain *then and there* of tomorrow.

Today is an acceptable time that the Lord has given us to live, and we must do so while we still have the ability. *Don't wait for tomorrow to start living today*. My favorite pastor, Rev. Dr. W. A. Blair, teaches and preaches, "Yesterday is a canceled check, tomorrow is a promissory note, today is cash in hand." Let us spend it wisely.

TIME FOR A NEW BEGINNING

It's quite understandable that the majority of black women are easily frustrated, doubtful, and insecure. We have been one of the least respected sectors of the American population. Not only have we experienced racial prejudices for being black, but we suffer sexual discrimination for being female. The negative images of blacks, portrayed by the media, are a major contributor to our feelings of despondency and hopelessness.

We have become so accustomed to news of crimes, drugs, diseases, and financial scarcity that our minds are now subconsciously programmed to expect the worst. This type of conditioning has formed pessimistic and unhealthy attitudes for too many African-Americans.

As deplorable as this process may be, it happens on a daily basis. There is no point in being annoyed or resentful—it won't help. The only way to get beyond these stumbling blocks is to empower ourselves, our children, and our households.

This empowerment begins with the greatest love of all—self-love. Self-love is not a selfish love but a "self-ful" love. A love that is full of self-appreciation, self-approval, and self-acceptance. Only when we take responsibility for ourselves, and cultivate positive self-images regardless of the opinions of others, can we create effective and lasting changes.

To find the key to turn stumbling blocks into stepping-stones, we must venture beyond our physical boundaries, beyond the walls of set standards, confinement, and limited controlled knowledge, and open the door to our *superconscious thinking.* We can then eliminate our fears and reprogram our minds to fulfill our individual desires.

The purpose of superconscious thinking is to find solutions to our problems. But we must allow it to work for us. We were never taught in school how to use our greater spiritual mind—only our physical, conscious mind. We learned our ABCs, reading, writing, and arithmetic, but not the power of superconscious thinking.

Superconscious thinking is using your greater mind instead of the everyday conscious mind. It is the ability to elevate your thought patterns to a higher level by tapping into your intuition anytime you choose to. Superconscious thinking is made up of a threefold process of meditation, visualization, and affirmation. I'll give you more details further along in this chapter.

PUT YOUR BEST FOOT FORWARD

In all my training programs, I emphasize that every day thousands of us come up with creative ideas. These ideas are interesting and important. But we ignore them. If we heard the same ideas from others, we would readily accept them. We wrongly *underestimate* the value of our own thinking, while we falsely *overestimate* the thinking of others.

Most people have more respect for others than they do for themselves. They wish they were in someone else's body, job, or lifestyle. This explains why so many people surrender to the dictates of others. We frequently allow another person to run our lives because we are afraid of losing that person's love. So we sacrifice our own feelings in favor of his or hers.

This type of existence creates psychological, spiritual, and physical disharmony. We shy away from making decisions because we are too concerned about what other people may think of our choice. We allow these self-limiting fears to control how we govern ourselves, destroying our creativity, curiosity, and spontaneity. If you think about this in depth, sis, you'll see that it prevents you from getting where you want to go, having the kind of fun you want to have, and doing the things you want to do.

Most people are fearful because they wrongly believe they "are not good enough," but some are afraid of being seen as "better than." They believe that if they excel at what they do, people may resent them; or that if they express their creative ideas, others may think they are "showing off."

DARE TO BE DIFFERENT

Listen, sis, for too long we have cramped our abilities and belittled our self-worth. This is a new millennium—and it's time for a new program. If you feel you have to deny your creativity in order to be accepted, you should change the company you keep. The simple truth is that some people are contemptuous of anyone who dares to be original. It's easy to criticize—anyone is capable of criticizing. But to come up with effective solutions is a different story.

Let me bring this home with a little biblical wisdom. "When men light a candle and put it on a candlestick instead of under a bushel, it gives light to all who are in its company. Let your light shine so bright before men, that they may see your good works and glorify your Creator which is in heaven."

You can read the entire teaching in Matthew 5. We must choose friends and associates who will let our light shine by respecting our thinking, enhancing our growth, and exchanging stimulating ideas. In *10 Bad Choices That Ruin Black Women's Lives,* I urged sisters to "drop the deadweight and go for the heavyweight" in love relationships. This advice doesn't apply only to love relationships but to every aspect of your life. This is your time to live, and live well, sis. Don't waste your time and energy weighing yourself down with other people's negative loads. Drop the deadweight, and start moving up to the next spiritual level in life. Amen!

RAISE YOUR VALUE BY RAISING YOUR LEVEL OF THINKING

To free ourselves to think on a superconscious level, we must get rid of our imagined fears. Fear is faith in reverse: faith is positive belief, while fear is negative belief. The only way we can overcome most fears is to do exactly what we are afraid of. For instance, if you're afraid of meeting new people, deliberately force yourself to do so in social settings. Practice being the first to introduce yourself to others. Before making your approach, give yourself a little pep talk like the following: "This usually scares me, but I'm going to do it. I may feel uneasy at first, because I'm not conditioned to do so, but I'm going to start right now. Why should I be intimidated by him/her, who's just another human being like me?" Practice doing this until you learn to be at ease when meeting people.

If you're fearful of asking questions, ask them anyway. Sis, no question is ever stupid. Asking a question is the only way to get an answer. This may sound extremely simplistic, but it's so true.

If you're afraid of public speaking, practice in front of friends, or join a local toastmaster's club. If you're fearful of your appearance for whatever reason, reread "Good Choice #1: Embracing the Skin You're In," and follow the beauty tips I shared. The point is to conquer whatever is hindering you from being your best self.

Who God Blesses Will Not Tarry in Messes

The sister who acknowledges herself as the manager of her life is a successful person. God is the owner; you are the manager. He has entrusted you with the care of your own life because He knows you can do it. God never gives us more burdens than we can bear. When times get rocky (and they will), call on Him to endow your superconscious mind with the answer to problems and challenges (and He will). A good manager takes responsibility for all her successes, as well as for her setbacks. She does not blame other people, hard times, or bad luck for her circumstances.

Self-Expression Is an Excellent Remedy

When negative thoughts visit us, we must question why we have those thoughts. Our minds absorb and react to whatever we put into them. That is why it is so important to get rid of our fears. We must find positive images to replace all of them. Negative and depressing thoughts come from many sources, including other people. Too many black women's psychological houses have been invaded by what I call the "Pression" family. Let's see, you have Auntie Depression, Uncle Oppression, Brother Repression, and Sister Suppression. As if these illegitimate squatters weren't enough of a hindrance, the "Session" neighbors sometimes decide to pay an unexpected visit—that's Mr. Obsession and Ms. Possession.

Sis, are any of these invaders dwelling in your mind or knocking at your door? I tell you what—it's eviction time. Time to clean house. Get your Spiritual Owner—the Almighty Landlord, God—to drive them out. Jesus promised this in John 14:18: "I will not leave you comfortless; I will come to you." The only "Pression" or "Session" that should be controlling your mind is your own Self-Expression.

YOU'VE GOT TO BELIEVE TO RECEIVE

Whenever fear enters, we must think: "I am free of all fear that exists now and in the future." My favorite affirmation, which I repeat many times throughout this book, is: "I am guided and protected in every way by Divine powers (of God)."

Anything our minds can believe, we can achieve. Please read this again: *Anything our minds can believe, we can achieve.* Jesus states this fact in Mark 9:23: "If you can believe, all things are possible to him that believe."

If you sincerely believe you'll have financial success, you will.
If you sincerely believe you'll have fulfilling love, you will.
If you sincerely believe you'll have peace of mind, you will.
If you sincerely believe you'll have good health, you will.

Whatever your mind can believe, you can achieve. This is the well-guarded Conceive, Believe, Achieve (CBA) secret, which was known to the "old boys' network," used by the privileged few, and passed down through many ages, but not taught in any classroom. Do not take it lightly. Use it passionately to empower your life, sis. Too many of us are depriving ourselves and prematurely dying because of a negative mindset.

Realize the power in this truth: If we can *conceive* the thought in our minds, and can *believe* it with all our hearts, then we can surely *achieve* it in our lives. The only catch is, you can't use it to try to control other people's minds against their wills. It won't work. For example, sis, you can't mentally force a particular person to love you. But you can use it to make yourself self-assured, embraceable, and desirable, so that the right person will find his way into your life.

A Superconscious Thinking Lesson
from "The Greatest"

All solutions are within us—we need not look for them outside. We need only to unfold our superconscious thinking and let it work for us, because "greater is he that is within us, than he that is in the world."

One of the earliest examples of this that I encountered was that of Muhammad Ali, former heavyweight boxing champion of the world. When I was twelve years old, my uncle, Robert Owen, who was a very close associate of Ali's, took my sister Angie and me to the champ's home in Cherry Hill, New Jersey. This was the first time we had met. His personality, as presented by the media, had always fascinated me. Upon meeting him, not being shy, I decided to ask him something I had always been curious about.

"Uncle Ali," I inquired, "why do you boast so much?" This amused him very much, and he laughed wholeheartedly. I'm not sure if it was the way I asked it or the question itself that he found so very funny. In a jovial manner, he responded:

I get in the ring, I dance and sing,
I open my mouth, I psych them out,
They look around and I knock them down,
For I AM THE GREATEST!

Muhammad Ali implanted in his superconscious thinking that he was "The Greatest"; therefore, in his conscious mind and to the rest of the world (including me), he became the greatest. What's particularly fascinating and amazing about this creative genius is the fact that in the ring he wasn't always the biggest, the strongest, or the fastest, but he was certainly the greatest. He has permanently carved his unique niche in history and in our hearts.

Whatever you conceive on the spiritual plane will eventually manifest itself on the physical plane. We must not confuse *wishing* and *believing*. A *wish* is the surface, conscious mind; it merely entertains us, with no true power to manifest itself. A *belief* stems from the very depth of our supersconcious thinking, and actually brings about changes in our lives.

YOU CAN FIND OIL ONLY WHEN YOU DRILL SOME WELLS

Succeeding in life doesn't always come easy. It takes a lot of persistence, perseverance, and courage. At times you'll feel as if it's hopeless. On some days, you may not be able to see the "light at the end of the tunnel." On other days, you'll cry like a baby. But no matter how discouraged you may be at times, sis, *do not give up.* Success may not come overnight, but it does come—if you're determined to win. This is a given fact: *You will win, sis.* If you keep knocking at a door, it is bound to open. Either someone is going to hear your knock and let you in, or it will eventually fall off the hinges from your constant banging—but it *will* open. "A winner never quits, and a quitter never wins!"

Sis, please trust me with this. If it weren't true, I wouldn't have shared it with you. I've spent a lifetime learning these lessons by direct application. *I wasn't born empowered, but I was born to be empowered.* At sixteen, I left home for college, paid my own way, took care of myself, and have been the manager of my own life ever since.

It wasn't always easy—I've gone through some fires and have been burned by many flames. But I kept going. I made up my mind that I was going to make it. I was going to make it without ever having to sleep my way there or step on anyone to get to where I planned to go. And I never did—praise God. Sis, it was not luck or coincidence that helped me through the turbulence and many storms. It was (and still is) my simple *belief and acceptance* of the comfort that Christ Jesus promised, which kept me comforted and opened me to a spiritual level of superconscious thinking. Use it to empower your life, and the people in your life. You are my sister, and I care. At this moment, I'm praying that whoever is reading this is being prepared and blessed by God most abundantly. "The race doesn't always go to the strongest or to the swiftest, but to the one who endureth."

How to Think Your Way into Winning

Superconscious thinking is a threefold process. It is built upon the foundation of:

Meditation—finding out what you want
Visualization—seeing the image in your mind
Affirmation—ordaining through the spoken word

To make this process work for you, you must peacefully accept that "if you have faith as tiny as a mustard seed, nothing shall be impossible unto you." Don't doubt it, just *know* that you deserve it. You must live your life with *expectation;* expect your mind to perform any task you ask of it. Once your mind gives you the solution, *focus* on it and make every *effort* to materialize it.

You will get what you desire because *focus plus effort equals manifestation.* Give thanks to God, and accept this powerful truth: "For whatsoever thing you desire, pray as if you already received it, and you shall surely have it."

The Threefold Process to Superconscious Thinking

MEDITATION

Meditation is one of the most useful, oldest, and simplest processes available to us. In some traditions, it is used for worship. In others, it is used as a method to achieve self-knowledge. In today's psychology, it is being used as a therapeutic method. Yet when most people hear the word *meditation,* they automatically think of some esoteric or difficult system.

Our society has made meditation seem like some mystical discipline that is difficult to practice. Some people do practice some complicated forms of meditation through various ritualized mantras and specialized breathing techniques, but meditation is only *a state of relaxed thinking.* And thinking is as natural to human beings as breathing, eating, and sleeping.

Meditation requires no force, struggle, or strain. To meditate, you don't need any special type of training, equipment, talent, experience, personality, status, or education. All you need is to be your natural self, to concentrate on what is going on inside of you, and to become uninvolved with your outside surroundings for the moment. You simply need to become relaxed.

When we meditate, we open and lift up our conscious thinking to a higher level, allowing ourselves to reach a state of tranquillity. This is a very peaceful state where all confusion disappears. We are able to tune in to our higher spiritual selves and know the *how, why, what,* and *where* of everything.

Relaxation is very important to our well-being and to the achievement of our desires. When we relax, we can think clearly about exactly what we want in our lives. We are then able to follow through with visualization and affirm our beliefs into reality.

Mediation is also very beneficial to us physically because when we are in a state of relaxation, there is no room for *anxiety, despondency,* or *frustration*—three of the major causes of mental dis-ease that leads to physical disease in the human body.

When you first begin to meditate, choose a time when you will not be disturbed. You can meditate anywhere: lying on your bed, sitting on the floor, soaking in your bathtub, or sitting under a tree. Just close your eyes and take a few deep breaths. Become peaceful, comfortable, and calm. Ask yourself anything you need to know. Some answers will come right away; others will take a little longer. Once you receive the answers to your inquiries, do not act immediately. There are many solutions to any one problem. Pray for proper guidance in order to be sure that the answer is ideal for you. The right one will consistently stand out. With this type of programming, you're now exposed to the center of your intuition. You can listen to your inner voice—the still, small voice of all wisdom and understanding: "Let those with ears, hear."

At some point, scattered thoughts and feelings may start to emerge in your mind. The more you rely on a higher level of thinking, the more sensitive your awareness becomes of all existing vibrations. Don't try to fight these scattered thoughts— just keep yourself relaxed and centered on the object of your meditation.

Only your ego on the conscious level is capable of giving life to the scattered thought by reacting to them. If you do not extend any effort, they will eventually float away because they have no active energy to exist on. Therefore, relax your ego, and let it surrender to your spiritual thoughts.

Believe that you *are* and can *do* and can *have* whatever you desire—that you stand at the doorway of your *higher self.* Through the persistent use of meditation, in conjunction with visualization and affirmation, you just have to "knock and it shall be opened unto you."

VISUALIZATION

Visualization is the act of envisioning what we want to happen. It's the act of using our imagination to create scenes that we desire in our lives. We form pictures in our minds all the time, when we daydream. By visualizing, we can tailor our daydreams to our specific wants. A want could be anything—a certain type of relationship, a situation, object, career, or goal. There's no limit to what we can create in our mind's eye.

Here are three easy and effective steps to creative visualization:

1. *Imagine the thing or situation that you wish to manifest.* For example, if you'd like a new place of residence, picture the house or apartment you'd like to have. Try to see it clearly. The image

may be unclear at first, but continue to relax and focus on your new place until it becomes vivid.

2. *See the thing or image already existing in the most perfect way.* Picture yourself moving around your new home. Walk through the rooms. Observe the color, furnishings, and decorating style you've chosen. See yourself perfectly comfortable in your new dwelling. It is very important that you see what you desire as *already existing.* Learn to adjust yourself to *feel it, sense it, see it,* and *accept it.*

3. *Give thanks.* Embrace your visualization with love. You must be persistent in order for it to materialize. Some desires may manifest instantly, while others may take some time. Continue with all your heart to "seek, and ye shall surely find."

AFFIRMATION

An affirmation is any statement, positive or negative, that we say or think. It is a declaration of acceptance. Whatever we accept about ourselves, we eventually become. Too often we continually make negative affirmations to ourselves and others, like "Just the thought of it *makes me sick*" or "I *hate* the way I look." These negative statements cause disharmony in our lives and hinder our growth.

When we repeatedly affirm anything, it becomes impressed in our minds and therefore becomes capable of molding our thoughts, which form the situations in our lives. If you periodically experience neck pains, nervousness, or exhaustion, by all means get it professionally checked out, but sis, please pay close attention to the sound vibrations you're sending out to the universe. Have you been uttering, "He is a *pain in the neck*" or "She *gets on my nerves*" or "I *can't stand* this job anymore"? Your own words can either be a wand or a weapon. Please use them to bring good to you.

The following easy affirmation technique will help you achieve your individual desires:

1. *Always affirm in the present tense.* You should never affirm in the future tense. For instance, you shouldn't declare, "I will be happy" or "I will have peace of mind." Instead say, "I am now happy" or "I am now at peace with myself." Our minds are such obedient and efficient servants that if we make declarations in the future tense, they'll be "there," not "here" in the present.

2. *Always declare positive statements.* For example, don't say, "I am not sick" or "I am not insecure." Instead say, "I am perfectly healthy" or "I am secure in all areas of my life."

3. *Always affirm with absolute intensity, conviction, and feeling.* Don't merely recite or mumble your affirmation. Sis, pour all your belief and desire into what you're stating. Don't be timid; be bold! Don't just hope, wish, or want, but *demand, command, ordain*—order your requests into present reality.

Many people, the first time they ever affirmed with conviction, broke right through the door that was obstructing their inherent gift. Not only did they *believe,* but they *knew* and *felt* the actuality of what they were ordaining. They didn't doubt or question it, they *evoked* and *accepted* it. Their minds were convinced of their spoken words.

The human mind is a beautiful instrument. It can be programmed for victory or defeat, wealth or poverty, love or hate, joy or misery—good or bad choices. It is there to serve us, sis. Always declare peace, perfection, and prosperity.

Open yourself to your superconscious thinking by requesting abundance and totality. Affirm exactly what you want, and let it manifest through your unwavering power of concentration and belief. Continue to "ask, and it shall be given unto you."

good choice #5

Avoiding "the Only Fly in the Buttermilk" Thinking

In my Father's house are many mansions.
John 14:2

Why aren't more blacks trying to lift each other up instead of pull each other down? So many sisters have confided in me about the "awful things we do to each other" in the workplace, in social settings, and in public.

For the promotion of *10 Bad Choices That Ruin Black Women's Lives,* I toured more than twenty major cities. It was a phenomenal experience. Happily, I have met and become good friends with some wonderful, kind, and supportive sisters across the country. But in three prime radio interviews in three major cities, the host couldn't get beyond "Bad Choice #1: Sisters Dissin' Sisters," because the phone kept ringing off the hook with sisters calling to share "the dirt" that other sisters had dissed them.

Overall the interviews went very well, because we were able to get the negative out in the open, in order to find positive solutions. But I have to tell you that I was very disappointed that so many sisters do such awful stuff to each other—all because of petty jealousy, insecurity, and wanting to be the first and only in any given situation. What's extremely sad is that this practice is completely unnecessary, because there is enough of everything for everyone if they apply themselves accordingly.

LET'S SEPARATE THE TRAUMA FROM THE DRAMA

This is a new millennium—it is time for the "token black" mentality to be an issue of the past. Instead of black women silently belittling each other, let's openly attempt to "walk a mile in each other's shoes" and try to understand that we are all works in progress.

And let's stop this nonsense about separating and dividing ourselves into cliques based on physical characteristics. The "field Negro" and "house Negro" psychological conditioning from the days of slavery must be catapulted back into the past and remain there for all eternity. To my darker-skinned sisters: Realize that it is no prize to be told, "At least you're pure and not confused." And to my lighter-skinned sisters: Acknowledge that it is no compliment to be told, "At least you're not too dark and can be accepted a little better."

These disturbing utterances—along with "good hair versus bad hair," "thin lips versus thick lips," "straight nose versus broad nose," and the "brown paper bag" and "ruler" tests—have sliced and diced the sister-community for too long. God did not create us to be Caucasian clones or chocolate-covered white women.

SOME FOLKS JUST DON'T GET IT

During one of my seminars in Los Angeles, "Stop Fretting and Start Getting Your Share of Success," Andrea, a thirty-four-year-old computer analyst, shared this with me: "I flew in from Cincinnati for the business expo, and when I heard you were in town, I had to come to your seminar. I'm glad I did because it's so good to see so many goal-oriented and positive black women together in one room. I had an experience on the plane that I couldn't believe. I was seated next to a white male executive. I was working on my laptop, and he kept peeking at me through the corner of his eyes. Finally, curiosity got the best of him and he asked, 'So what do you do?' I told him. As fate would have it, we had the same profession.

"He looked as if he were a little uneasy and kept asking me a lot of questions: where did I go to school, what was my training, which company do I work for. I answered all his questions, but he kept pressing: 'Are you very good at it, or just making your way through it?' I looked directly at him and told him that my company seemed to think that I was good because they promoted me twice within the last five years. This must have really gotten to him, because then he started speaking to me in technical language. He spurted out all sorts of technological inquiries, as if he were trying to test me. When I matched his wit and used technical terms to answer him, he really looked puzzled. After being scrutinized for about an hour, I got tired and fell asleep.

"I must have napped only for about half an hour or so when he actually woke me up just to say, 'You know, I've been thinking. You must be among the top five percent in your race. There can't be many more of you.' I couldn't believe he said that to me. I didn't know what to think, but I didn't allow myself to get mad. I asked him how many black people he had taken time to get to know, and I told him that I was more the norm than the exception in my race. He didn't say much after that. I think I left him with a new view of African-Americans."

DESIRE TO INSPIRE OTHERS TO RESPECT YOU

I'm glad Andrea didn't get mad—it wouldn't have solved anything. She acted wisely by stating clearly and precisely what black people are about today. If any African-American takes a statement like the one Andrea heard as a compliment, she is doing both herself and her race a great disservice. Although innocently shared and honestly meant, it should be corrected. Simply, in a polite manner, thank the person for the kind effort, but let them know that you are very much black and just one of very many who do not fit the negative stereotypical image of African-Americans.

This is meant not to belittle well-meaning folks or potential peers but to help to educate them. If you are to be true friends, you must be able to communicate openly with each other, or else the friendship or acquaintanceship will be built on sheer hypocrisy.

I have friends from all walks of life and from all different backgrounds. I love my sisters (and brothers) dearly, from the darkest to the lightest and the thirty-six shades in between. I interact with a wide variety of associates, from those who sweep the boardrooms, to those who run the boardrooms, to those who own the boardrooms. If and when stereotypes become an issue, I set the record straight immediately.

As a matter of fact, twelve years ago, when I first met one of my now-close Jewish girlfriends, Linda, in the Hamptons, one of the first things she said was, "To me you're not black, you are brilliant."

This did not sit well with me at all. Sis, I admit I snapped at her, "Oh, no you don't! Don't you dare try this divide-and-conquer psychology with me! I love my race, and I'm very proud to be a black woman." She sincerely apologized, and I told her I accepted her apology, but "if we're going to be true friends, don't ever make a statement like that to me again." Over the years we have matured, diversified, and learned a lot about each other's culture.

True friends and well-meaning people will be grateful to you for pointing out prejudice—which is prejudgment—because they probably don't understand the impact of negative statements such as these. They too are victims of a psychological conditioning inherited from their forefathers.

All their lives white Americans have been led to believe, either silently or openly, that being the offspring of the governing group in America assures them a psychological edge over other ethnic groups. If their beliefs have not been corrected, then being exposed to blacks who are just as beautiful, intelligent, articulate, or successful can and does throw their thinking off its superficially programmed path. In other words, while the members of the governing group have been falsely conditioned to believe that they are "better than," the majority of blacks have been subliminally programmed to believe that they are "less than."

GOD CREATED ALL IN HIS IMAGE—EQUAL!

The Universal Truth is, no race or individual is superior to another. The beauty of this truth lies within the power of the human mind. *No particular race has better brains that another; success depends on discipline and purpose.* If we would only learn to effectively use our superconscious thinking, then struggling for approval and equality would be issues of the past.

We must become aware of our individual obstacles and develop plans to overcome them. We are strong, intelligent, and capable beings. We have achieved much, but we still need to accomplish much more. Until African-Americans, individually and collectively, learn how to empower themselves and respect each other, we will always be subject to the dictates of a governing group outside of our ethnic group. It's that simple.

God has given all humans the same gift of *free will.* We all house it in our body temples. We are all the same, equal in the eyes of our Creator, who commanded from the very beginning, "Let us make man in our own image." Unfortunately, human beings throughout time have used the powerful gift of the mind to outwit and subdue each other. The Hebrews were subjugated by the Egyptians, the Jews by the Germans, the Koreans by the Japanese, and the Africans by the Europeans. God has always supplied a guide to lead each group from bondage to freedom— whether that be freedom of the mind, body, or spirit.

Blacks in America had a fine example in Dr. Martin Luther King, Jr., who was guided by the loving and peaceful teachings of

Jesus. We have surely come a long, long way, sis. Unfortunately, we are still somewhat scattered because we tend to be an ego-oriented group.

Let's Talk about Unity in the Sista Community

Once we have reached a certain level of status, we are quick to separate ourselves from the fellow brother or sister who is still trying to find his or her way along the path. We have this need to prove that we are "better than" our very own brother or sister. We spend so much unnecessary time trying to show that we look, dress, act, buy, or drive "better than" our fellow black siblings. The workplace becomes a major battleground: in our attempt to be the "only fly in the buttermilk," we indulge in office gossip, backbiting, and mud-slinging.

The author of an *Essence* article, "How Black Women Wound One Another—And How We Can Stop," wrote, "Even at an event like the Million Woman March, which was supposed to bring us together in solidarity and sisterhood, we divided along class lines, the well-heeled and established folks dissing the grass-roots organizers and vice versa."

Women of color must take the initiative to respect and appreciate each other in spite of our differences. If we don't put away the petty nonsense and get our acts together soon, we may be heading for a very desolate future.

Until each and every black woman, man, and child can walk and dwell in any corner of the United States of America peacefully and safely, we are all affected, either directly or indirectly, regardless of who we are.

Let's get our acts together and try to understand each other's experience and free ourselves from intraracial prejudice.

Avoid the Three Self-defeating C's

Overall, when sisters of color deal with issues on a one-to-one basis, a special tie bonds them. But when a third force comes into play—be it a man, money, or a certain position—some women begin to discredit each other's worth, sensing competition. Let us acknowledge right now that there is no "real" competition in life. It's all an illusion, for "what is truly yours cannot be taken away."

In my national seminars, I tell sisters to make sure they never get sidetracked in life by "the three self-defeating C's": *competing, copying,* and *comparing.* These are misleading values that our society encourages. Instead of thinking, "I have to keep up with the Joneses" or "I have to look better than Jane Doe," shouldn't we each be declaring, "I must be the best that I can be"? If we would all concentrate on being our best individual selves, we would have no time to compare, copy, or compete with our sisters, brothers, or persons from any other ethnic race. We would strive to help instead of hinder each other.

The plain truth is, we are all passengers on this oversize boat called Earth. And whether we sink or survive depends on how well we can paddle together. If one of us should fall overboard, who will rescue her? If all are selfish, she will drown. But if a spirit of sisterhood prevails, one of our crew members will gladly rescue our sister. Life is not a one-woman cruise. Our Divine Creator is the only captain of this ship.

Sis, help me out here. Why is it that we of black descent do not take a more active role in promoting each other's ideas, businesses, trades, and endeavors? If we do not think enough of ourselves to patronize each other's businesses, how can we expect other ethnic groups to do so?

I do not intend in any way to imply that we should confine ourselves, our friendships, our relationships, or our spending power to our own ethnic group. No, we live in a multicultural society, and it's important to interact, learn, and grow with other cultures. But let us not neglect the very rich and beautiful culture that is our very own.

Behind the masks we wear—blacks, whites, Asians, Indians, and Hispanics—we are all the same deep within. We are all human beings trying to make it in this world, to be fulfilled in our friendships and relationships, and to earn enough money to live without worry.

THE MORE FAMILIAR WE BECOME, THE MORE SIMILAR WE SEEM

Because of their ignorance of Divine Love, human beings have foolishly divided themselves by their outer shells. But there are no intrinsic differences between people. We vary only in our upbringing, experiences, and basic guidance.

It is truly beyond any reasonable comprehension that people can actually dislike each other simply because of the color of their skins, the texture of their hair, or the size of their bank account. If we could spiritually uplift ourselves and realize that we are all the same beyond these flesh temples—and embrace each other for who we are instead of how we look and what we have—our lives would be so much more peaceful and delightful.

We cannot prevent other ethnic groups from throwing discriminating remarks at us, but we can, love, respect, and appreciate ourselves to the extent where such statements have no impact.

Everyone is entitled to his or her opinions. We can't stop people from prejudging. Although it may not be right, it is done. Each and every one of us, at some point or another, has been guilty of prejudging others. Therefore we shouldn't condemn others for their prejudices—but we don't have to accept or believe them, either.

Here's a Universal Truth we can all learn from:

There is so much good in the worst of us,
And so much bad in the best of us,
That it hardly behooves any of us
To talk about the rest of us.

First printed in the *Marion* (Kansas) *Record,* owned by Governor Edward Wallis Hoch [1849–1925]; assumed to have been written by him.

We must all try to live harmoniously with each other. But if we sisters do not care for each other, who will care for us? This doesn't mean we have to tolerate every black person, just because they happen to be black. Not by any means. If anyone causes you discomfort or harm, you must remove yourself from that person's reach. But in general, let's spread some compassion toward each other as sisters and realize how important it is to form meaningful friendships.

A very good friend of mine, Sonia Alleyne, editor-in-chief of *Black Elegance* and *Belle* magazines, is one the most supportive sisters I know. "When you have a good friend in your corner, it makes the rough spots in life less difficult," she once told me. "Supportive friends are a blessing at all times. They laugh with us, cry with us, share our victories, our mishaps, our breakups, and our new relationships. They stick with us through thick and thin. No one can take the place of a really good sister-friend."

HEAL A SISTER, HEAL A FUTURE

A new growth of sister-circles, reading groups, and prayer groups are springing up throughout the country. They're good, sis. You should either join one or start one. It is important to form genuine, meaningful, and trustworthy friendships with other sisters. You can start with just a few people if necessary and meet once a week or twice per month—whatever your schedule permits.

If we each would brighten up a little corner where we live from day to day, that would be enough to increase our society's respect toward black women. If each of us would just influence five people in her lifetime, and they in turn influence five more, and so on, this would be a new dawning. A positive vibration would be created—an electrical current, spreading like spiritual wildfire, from one sister to another.

We would see our ideas materialize and our dreams be achieved. It would be a better world for ourselves and for future generations.

I believe:

If you can heal a black woman, you can heal a black child
If you can heal a black child, you can heal a black community
If you can heal a black community, you can heal a black future

GIVE A CHILD NEW HOPE

Black children need positive role models.

Cultural pride must be instilled in them from an early age. But when people are hungry, they don't want to hear about culture. Our youths need to be nourished today. One of our chief problems is scarcity—inadequate food, housing, and education. Scarcity and want deprive the mind of functional thought. They reduce people to the level of beasts. They lead to destruction and hate.

If a man is full, he will not harm another in order to gain, because he already has. He will not think of shooting his own brother, or anyone else, or pushing drugs for a "quick dollar."

We live in a very competitive society. We have been programmed to believe that our rise, fall, or survival depends on how skillfully or cunningly we can outdo each other—how well we "beat the competition." We must strive to be our individual best, but not by competing or "beating" down others.

Materialism plays a very important role in black awareness. If a man is without shelter, or a woman cannot pay her bills, how can either of them listen to and pass on information about the healing of a race? How can a hungry child learn? How can a distraught personality function? What we need to know, what our mates and our children need to know, is that they do matter.

Our black youths are drowning in their neighborhoods. They are dying for an image. Limited exposure to the finer things in life, as advertised in magazines and films and on television, has led them to anger, frustration, and aggression. One reason black youths today are entertained by guns is that guns give them a feeling of power. For instance, a young black boy from an under-privileged background sees designer jackets, jeans, and all-star sneakers being promoted as the "in" thing that will make him "the new man on the block." Being from the ghetto, he cannot afford to pay for this image. His gun now becomes his means to get "in," to become "the man." This is very ugly, and it needs to stop now.

As we all know, our country is stimulated by scandal. The media can be very damaging. Negative publicity plays and stays in people's minds. What may be entertaining to a small group can be discrediting to an entire race. If the media would stop playing up all the negative issues, some of this violence would cease.

The spirit is being taken out of black youths today. If the mass population does not accept them, how are they to function? Our youths are crying for help. There are too many children out there who need to be properly guided, cherished, and nurtured.

Providing that care is a major challenge, but we have to start somewhere. We may not be able to guide the older ones, but we can start by training the younger ones for the future. *Train up a child in the way he should go, and when he is old, he will not depart from it.*

EACH ONE, REACH ONE

Sis, today we need a total awareness, from both the educated and the noneducated classes, to reverse the downfall of the black race. Separating ourselves based on our skin complexions is ugly. We are all connected. One sector of the population, directly or indirectly, affects the other sectors.

The varying shades of skins don't matter—the main issue is our behavior patterns. We must come together to find effective solutions. Superconscious thinking can furnish solutions to all problems. Let us use it wisely. Instead of looking outside for change, waiting to "get a break," or hoping for things to get better, the black community has to make an effort from within. We must empower our kids and teach them how to live in the present and prepare for bright futures. Sister-circles, churches, and prayer groups are excellent foundations to initiate youth-empowerment programs.

THE TEN-STEP YOUTH EMPOWERMENT PROGRAM

Step 1. Get youths to stop comparing, copying, and competing with each other.

Step 2. Reach underprivileged youths, and encourage their participation in trade and institutional training.

Step 3. Replace the outrageous, ruthless, and self-destructive behavior of many black youths with manners, self-respect, and respect for society in general.

Step 4. Stop the killing, robbing, and beating of blacks, by blacks and other ethnic groups.

Step 5. Replace hunger, homelessness, and illiteracy with proper food, shelter, and education.

Step 6. Protect children from abuse and incest.

Step 7. Create books, and ensure proper teaching in the classrooms.

Step 8. Develop the superconscious thinking of black children.

Step 9. Understand and apply the true meaning of the teachings of God.

Step 10. Ensure that all of the above are built on a solid foundation that will last throughout our lifetime and future generations.

These issues need to be addressed by collective effort. "It takes a village to raise a child" is a well-known African proverb. We must all champion this cause. When we have a sense of community, racial slurs, by other ethnic groups as well as our own, will be meaningless, and our self-worth will remain unshaken.

Sis, don't strive to be a "token black," or "the only fly in the buttermilk." Join a positive sister-circle, or an enterprising black women's organization, coalition, or social club, because "a wire standing alone is easily broken, but many wires bound together, into a cable, are not easily bent."

good choice

#6

Trusting Your Own Intuition

*And thine ears shall hear
a word behind thee saying,
This is the way, walk ye in it.*
Isaiah 30:21

A very good business associate of mine, Angela, a thirty-four-year-old biracial sister, recently called me on the verge of tears. We had known each other for a little over three years, but she had never divulged the intricacies of her family background. She called to ask me about a dating dilemma she was facing.

Angela has a very successful marketing business, and she was at the point in her life where she would like to meet an ideal partner and get married. The first year I met her, she dated black men exclusively. Her father is black and her mother is white. If a white man asked her out, she refused him without a second thought. But by the second year, and after a few heartbreaks (from bad choices), she changed her taste from black men to white. These were her very words: "I'm tired of being used by black men. I want to meet and marry a nice white guy."

I explained to her that it was not my place to agree or disagree with her decision, especially since she belongs to both races—no one had the right to judge her choice. But I told her that she was wrong to judge all black men negatively due to the bad apples she

had picked. Finding a mate isn't about a person's race, I empha-
sized; it's about his character, whether he is black, white, or other.

ONLY TIME CAN TRULY TELL

After a year of dating white men exclusively but finding no love
connection, she decided to date what she described as "upscale
men of both races"—doctors, lawyers, investment bankers, and
so on. The evening she called me, she said that she had met two
black men on a recent business trip to Michigan. Both were doctors. She agreed to go on a date with each of them. The first one
she really liked, but the second one, she said, she didn't care for
that much.

After not hearing from the first one, she decided to accept the
dating proposal from the second. By their fourth date, he was
seriously interested in dating her exclusively.

At this point in her story, she paused briefly.

"What's the matter?" I wanted to know.

"I asked him if he wanted kids," she answered.

"So soon?" I inquired. "Why? What did he say?"

"He said he would like to get married to someone like me and
have two or three children," Angela shared.

"That's a nice start," I complimented.

"No, it's not," said Angela. "I don't want kids. I am not going
to fall into that trap and bring kids into this world."

"What?" I asked, stunned. This is the first time she had
revealed this side of herself to me. I simply listened in silence and
mild shock as she continued: "I told him since he wanted kids, we
should not continue to see each other because I do not plan to
have any."

DR. CORNISH: What did he say?

ANGELA: He was surprised and hurt.

DR. CORNISH: Why did you say it was a "trap"? Why don't you want kids?

ANGELA: Because it is a vicious trap, and I just don't want to bring kids into this world.

DR. CORNISH: Are you sure you won't change your mind about children somewhere down the line?

ANGELA: No way!

DR. CORNISH: First of all, if you don't want kids, you should not be dating men who have never had children before—or else you're going to keep hurting people. Maybe you should concentrate on dating men who already have children, or divorced men, or older ones who don't want any kids.

ANGELA: I know. You're right. But I want a guy my age who's never been married.

DR. CORNISH: What if you meet such a man, and he already has children?

ANGELA: Then that's okay. As long as they aren't mine and they don't live with us.

DR. CORNISH: Angela, it's me. Tell me the truth. Why are you so against having children?

After about half an hour of hesitation, Angela finally opened up to me with tears. "My father is the cause," she blurted out. "When I was little, we lived in an almost all-white neighborhood. When my friends, who were white, would come over to play, he would always yell at me and ask, 'Aren't black kids good enough for you?' I didn't even realize the color difference until he made it an issue. I was just a child. Then when I started dating, he would constantly scold, 'Aren't black guys good enough for you? I don't want you bringing home any white boys.' What a hypocrite! He would tell my two younger brothers, 'Get a nice white girl like your mother.' He is so sick. And my mother is so weak, she wouldn't stand up to him for me. That's why I don't go home anymore, and that's why I don't want any kids. I don't want them mixed up like my family."

You've Got to Take Back Your Personal Power

After a brief pause, I comforted, "Angela, you are not responsible for where you came from. But you are responsible for where you are going. There is nothing wrong with you. What's wrong is your father's hypocritical mentality. He cannot choose for you. You are no longer a child who is subjected to his nonsense. You can run your own life. What you are is a beautiful gift from God. Don't ever doubt that. Don't hate your makeup. There are many interracial families who function beautifully, but unfortunately, your household was headed by a dysfunctional manager and a codependent spouse. That's not your fault.

"Your dad seems to have a dislike for black women, because he coached your brothers to avoid them. He is mentally flawed—but that's his problem. Not all black men are like that at all. Please don't judge brothers by your father's behavior. All you can do is pray for your parents and wish them the best. Try to reestablish a relationship with them, but stand up to them respectfully and firmly. Let them know how much they have hurt you. Tell them you want a loving relationship with them, but you will be running your own life and marrying whom you choose.

"Time has a way of changing people, if they have valuable experiences over the years. Maybe your dad has somehow gotten enlightened and has come to terms with his own self-hatred. It's quite possible that he has grown to realize that people are all beautiful—even he himself. If he still chooses to criticize you, then stay away, but please, don't let that stop you from having a beautiful family, with kids of your own. You can make it right for them—by teaching them unconditional love and accepting all people as the wonderful creations that God made."

After our conversation, Angela was relieved. She promised she would visit her family and consider having a future family, because deep down she really wanted one—and deserved to have one.

IF OTHERS DON'T LIKE YOUR DECISION—OH, WELL!

Criticism from others is nothing new. It's how you choose to handle it that really matters. Whenever you "dare to be different," you will be criticized for your uniqueness. Most people like, and feel at home with, conformity. They want you to conform to their average lifestyle, average choices, and average conversations. But you are not an average human being. Average people don't read empowerment books like this one. They are satisfied with their existence as it is. And there is nothing wrong with that—it is their personal choice. What's wrong, however, is for them to criticize you for daring to be different—for daring to be empowered.

What's even worse is for you to hinder or alter your life based on their definitions and expectations of how you should live and what you should do. Shame on you if you let one more day pass with the management of your life handed over to someone else.

Most people are quick to tell you how you should adapt to their way of life. They want you to dress, eat, decorate, and marry the same as they. If you don't, the gossip starts. Some people are simply nosy and jealous—it's a fact. What's extremely awful is, sometimes the criticism comes from those who are closest to you.

Being criticized by close associates is nothing new either. Moses, God's favorite servant in the Old Testament, was criticized by family because he married an Ethiopian sister. In Numbers 12, I read that God dealt sternly with the self-appointed critics because He cherished Moses. However, Moses asked God to forgive them. And He did. Sis, when someone criticizes you, don't belittle yourself. Remember Moses' example—refrain from anger and insecurity, and center yourself in the Lord's plan for your life.

WHERE GOD GUIDES, HE PROVIDES

When God calls you and presents Himself in you, your life is never the same again. Sis, God can be calling you at this very moment. You may not always know what God has planned for you—sometimes you can't see through the fog. But hold steadfast to this: Keep out the negative utterances out of your mind.

When people come buzzing around asking, "Who do you think you are?" or "What are you going to do?" or "How are you going to make it?" tell them, "I know who I am. But more important, I know *whose* I am. I am the daughter of God. And as sure as the sun will shine, I will make it, and I will not hide out of fear or shame, and I will not bury my head in the sand."

Sometimes it may seem as if God has forgotten about you—but trust me, He has not. He has a way of sometimes delivering at the eleventh hour, just in the nick of time. He wants to test you to see if you are using the gift and power of your superconscious thinking to get out of the pickle yourself. Sometimes you don't know how your bills are going to be paid—it may be in the middle of the month, and you have not yet seen the first dollar for your rent or mortgage that's due in only two weeks.

At are other times your car payment and phone and utility bills are backed up, and creditors are hounding you. Or you may want to finance a business or project and don't know where to start. Don't panic, sis. I have "been there, done that," and I will give you specific examples of overcoming these *temporary* setbacks in "Good Choice #7: Taking Calculated Chances, Not Idle Ones."

GET A HEAD START BY GETTING ON THE TRIPLE-A LIST

When problems seem to overpower you, make sure *you empower you* by being on God's A-list—*asking, accepting,* and *achieving.* Ask through prayer, accept by believing with unshakable faith, and achieve by taking action. Sis, start right where you are: "Take off your shoes, get vulnerable in front of God, because the place where you stand is Holy ground."

Throw off those old shoes and your knapsack full of errors. Don't be blinded by the folly of others, mistakes in judgment, or untrustworthy people. Don't be a dreamer of dreams, a victim of illusion and delusion, who awakens only when surrounded by danger, or when it's too late to rectify a situation or salvage a relationship. Become renewed and refreshed. Get rid of everything, and remove yourself from everyone who is holding you back and hindering your growth and success.

God is your Creator. He knows what is troubling you, but He wants you to acknowledge Him as center of your life. In Exodus 3:7–8, He says, "I have surely seen the affliction of my people, and have heard their cry by reason of their taskmasters; for I know their sorrow. I have come down to deliver them and bring them out of that land to a good land."

Are any taskmasters or dreary tasks causing you sorrow, sis? Whatever situation you're currently in, God is a very present help in all times of need. He never gives us more than we can bear. It's up to you to take the initiative by believing. God will trust you to manage your own life—so make sure you do it effectively by trusting your own intuition and following your hunches, and not handing over the run of your life to someone else.

YOU'VE GOT TO SPEAK UP IF YOU WANT TO BE HEARD

Once you decide to take charge of your life, who can decide how quickly or how slowly your individual empowerment will take place? The answer is—only you and God, in partnership together.

No one else on this earth can interfere with your progress, unless you wimp out and let them take charge.

This is true for every area of your life: the personal, romantic, social, financial, and professional. I did the following interview for *Black Enterprise* in its "Motivation and Peak Performance" section:

YOUR OPINIONS COUNT, TOO

"You've got to be vocal if you want to be respected in the workplace," says Grace Cornish, Ph.D., a social psychologist based in New York City. Cornish says that you can't allow other people's perceptions to keep you from saying what's on your mind. "If you do, you run the risk of appearing disinterested or looking like a doormat—two things you want to avoid at all costs in the office."

For professionals and entrepreneurs alike, a strong vocal presence is a powerful asset in the marketplace. If you need to increase yours, consider the following pointers from Cornish:

• **Make sure your work is on the money.** A clean attendance record and good performance evaluations will make your opinions shine that much brighter.

• **Know your stuff.** It's hard to argue with facts. "Do research so you have the factual ammunition to back up your personal insights," asserts Cornish.

• **Check your total image.** Whether you like it or not, you're judged by your appearance. Dress and carry yourself in a way that will demand respect and lend credence to whatever you say.

• **Affirm yourself.** It takes 21 days for a habit to set, says Cornish. So start telling yourself today that "what you have to say is important and worthwhile for others to hear."

What You Are Is Not Who You Are

Who you are, sis, is not *what* you are. Who you are is a daughter of God. What you are is:

- what you have been through
- what someone has done to you
- what someone says about you
- what you have accumulated
- what you own, drive, or wear
- what position you hold
- what education you have had

These are all examples of your *whatness,* not your *whoness.* Your *whatness* is from outside of your very essence. Your *whoness* is from within your very center. It is of God. Sis, you are a royal princess—a chosen vessel—the daughter of the Living God, the Life Force of the *I am.*

When I wrote the poem "Am I?" (on the dust jacket of *Radiant Women of Color*) in 1994, I sought to find a common theme that affected black women from varying educational, financial, and social backgrounds. I searched for something that we have all pondered about at one point or another. I purposely left the poem in question form so as to inspire conversation—to serve as a catalyst for healing, both silently and openly.

It is truly fascinating how many sisters have called, written, and approached me to say that they have used the poem as the opening theme in their discussion groups and workshops across the county.

> *AM I an innocent victim*
> *of an overdose of melanin*
> *or has the sun lovingly*
> *kissed my face*
> *and blessed me*
> *as part of this Negroid race?*

why do I experience
such perplexity
as I observe the reflection
of my skin complexion,
the texture of my hair,
the curve of my behind
the shape of my nose,
or the state of my mind?

have I been flawed by nature
as my European siblings
would have me believe
or am I the state of grace
our body temples are placed
on Earth to achieve?

what true wisdom
can enlighten my soul?
are the answers hidden
in the tombs of my mothers
of time past?
Isis, Makeda, Nefertiti, Cleopatra,
can your daughter's
thirst for understanding
be quenched at last?

EACH ONE, TEACH ONE

The poem "Am I?" has touched and inspired many lives. The following year, I was led to answer my own question, with "I Am." I published a limited run in 1995, and it too, received rave reviews. After listening, learning, and experiencing a tremendous spiritual growth, I have revised it as follows:

I AM the clay, perfectly molded
*   by the hands of the Universal Potter*
I am the salt of the earth
an incarnated mind, body and spirit
*   with a deliberately timed birth*

I am a purpose,
*   a song worth singing*
in the midst of all the worldly madness,
*   Earth-bound sadness*
I am the root that springs hope
*   of a New Testament gladness*

Peace . . . be still . . . listen to the faint rhythm
*   of the whispering voice within*
harmonics of the Creator
*   synchronizing to a sanctified sacred beat*
the silent song of Wisdom beckoning
*   her children to unleash Christ-like feat*

At the dawn of this awakening
the embracing of eternal truths
Father Time starts a planetary countdown
*   with his universal clock*
as Mother Earth fervently gathers
*   her enlightened flock*

O thou of little faith,
Penetrate the mystery of the MESSIAH
*   for HE IS SHE . . . SHE IS HE . . .*
HE IS SAME AS SHE, HIM, ME . . . we . . .
take heed my sisters, decode the riddle
*   of this wondrous anagram*
and know that all humans are . . .
*   . . . flesh temples of the I AM!*

Sis, there is a wise old saying: "When the student is ready, the teacher will appear." It is up to you to decide when you are ready to open yourself to the spirit of truth. I will discuss this awesome spiritual awareness in great depth with you in "Good Choice #10: Using Praying Energy for Staying Energy."

WHEN YOU'RE AN EAGLE, DON'T SCRATCH WITH CHICKENS

You must always trust in your own intuition. Do not let other people run your life. Many of the problems in our lives are caused by outside influences. We keep looking for outside information to fill us up, instead of seeking inside confirmation to lift us up.

This confirmation comes from God, our Creator—who is the living *I am*—not the "I was" or the "I will" but the present *I am*. God is a *now* God. He is alive and functioning in the present. You can call upon Him and decide to improve your life at any point in time. In Exodus 3:14, He described Himself to Moses as "I AM THAT I AM." He didn't say "I am that I was" or "I am that I will be."

He is alive and willing to nurture and comfort you today. Someone once said, "Today is only yesterday's tomorrow." Another said, "Yesterday is already gone, tomorrow is not here yet, today is a gift—and that's why they call it *the present*."

Accept your precious present from the *I am* today. When others try to run your life for you, or gossip about you, or backbite you in any way, smile, don't fret. And if you feel like answering, tell them, "*I am* capable of running my own life, because I trust my own intuition."

And trust me, your God-given intuition will work wonders for you. In her best-selling book, *Ladies First,* popular T.V. talk-show host and grammy award–winner Queen Latifah confirmed, "Everything that you are, everything that you can be, starts inside of you and it starts with God."

Well said, sis!

good choice #7

Taking Calculated Chances, Not Idle Ones

For which of you, intending to build a tower,
sitteth not down first, and counteth the cost,
whether he have sufficient to finish it?
Luke 14:28

Have you ever wondered why some people seem to master life's challenges effortlessly, while others seem to constantly struggle to get the same things accomplished?

I have an insider's secret for you: The former folks don't have it any easier than the latter. The truth is, seemingly effortless success is based on clever craftsmanship and execution of a triple-P formula: *product, promotion,* and *persistence*.

To get ahead in life, first you have to get to know your product—whether it's yourself, a business, an event, a record, or a book. Next, you must promote it well, by getting the word out to as many people as possible. Then, you have to be persistent, against all odds.

TO GET POSITIVE PROMOTION, GET INTO POSITIVE MOTION

Recently a fellow author and I were invited to appear on one of the highest-rated weekend radio shows. The topic was "Healing Male-Female Relationships." First the host introduced me and gave me ten minutes to briefly sum up the "ten bad choices that ruin Black women's lives." I shared them quickly and articulately because I knew my subject well. Next, she introduced the second guest, a novelist (let's call him Author #2), and gave him ten minutes to share the contents of his book. He took the first few minutes to explain why he wrote the book and the balance of his time to complain that his book wasn't selling well due to "the media not featuring him." Not once did he share the contents of his book. He just kept complaining about how "the media was unfair to him." The host politely interrupted him and took a quick commercial break.

After the break, the host announced, "This question is for both of you. Can you share how men can avoid making bad choices in relationships?"

AVOID THIS NEGATIVE ATTITUDE AT ALL COSTS

Author #2 volunteered in a very sarcastic tone, "I guess I will let the doctor answer that question, since you seem to be promoting her book more than mine." Both the host and I were surprised by his negative tone. But I jumped right in and quickly shared some of the "bad choices" men make in relationships and how they can avoid them.

The host and I had a lively conversation, while Author 2 pouted silently. He was foolishly throwing away valuable airtime because of a chip on his shoulder toward the media. To help him out, I inquired, "Author #2, in your introduction you said one of the reasons you wrote your book was because you wanted 'men to treat women with more respect.' I enjoyed reading your book. Will you share with our listeners some of the ways in which you addressed these issues?"

"Well, I would have done that from the beginning," he declared bitterly, "but she [the host] started talking about 'choices,' addressing you and ignoring me."

"I directed the question to both of you," said the host very graciously. "Will you join in and give us your view on how men can avoid making 'bad decisions' in relationships?"

Author #2 shared three brief tips, then switched back to his declaration of how "the media shuts him out." (I'm not kidding you, he kept hammering away at this.) The conversation continued in this manner:

AUTHOR #2: The media just keep closing the door in my face—

HOST: *[cutting in]* Listeners, can you please go out and buy Author 2's book?

AUTHOR #2: They [the media] won't give me my props. Just because I'm not some doctor, or I don't write nonfiction books, they won't put me on those talk shows. They won't feature me in those magazines, and nobody knows about my book, and that's why it's not selling.

DR. CORNISH: You should stop selling yourself short. If you just sit back and expect the media to come to you to promote your book, you are kidding yourself. It doesn't work like that. You have got to get out there and pursue the media. And if a door closes in your face, then find a window or some other opening to get through. Whether you're a doctor, actor, butcher, baker, or candlestick maker, if you're sharp and persistent, they will eventually feature you. But if you are not good at marketing yourself, you won't get very far.

AUTHOR #2: I'm a good brother, and my stuff isn't selling. Then the brothers who write trash, theirs sell like hotcakes. For example, there is this brother named—[He actually had the indecency to name and mudsling another brother over the radio.] He's on every show and best-seller list, and the media and readers just love his stuff, and it's all junk! The good guys don't get the breaks.

COMPLAINING IS DRAINING—GET INTO POSITIVE ACTION

DR. CORNISH: You have to create your own tailor-made breaks in
life. You don't get ahead by bashing others. You have to
have a product you believe in, then publicize the heck out of
it. For instance, I am on most of the major TV talk shows all
the time. Do you think they let me on because I am cute—
although I am? *[smile]* The reason I get on is because I
believe in my work enough to keep telling people about it in
a very positive way. I am lively, articulate, professional, and
most of all persistent. I have paid my dues in the past—
sometimes it took over a year of constant calls to get on *one*
show—but now I get so many offers that I sometimes have
to turn some down. It's not always easy, but I like what I do,
so I do it well. This also works well for magazines and
newspapers. I'm featured often because I have all the P's
covered—I have a good product, and I am professional,
polite, pleasant, patient, and persistent.

AUTHOR #2: I've tried, but I guess they don't like me.

DR. CORNISH: You know what? The best-selling tool within the
African-American market is word of mouth. Start doing
some local seminars and lectures in your area, get a buzz
going, and then branch out.

HOST: That's an excellent idea, Dr. Cornish. That's what you do,
isn't it? I see in your media kit that you do a lot of national
seminars and workshops.

AUTHOR #2: There we go again, I've tried that. You know, you
spend all this money, set a date and get a place, and only
about six or seven people show up—because the media
won't let me on to publicize my event.

DR. CORNISH: Enough! My dear, if you really have a deep love for what you are doing, you will find a way to get it out to as many people as possible. Use me as an example. I am on a serious mission to promote healthy dialogue between black men and women. I truly care, and I talk to just about everyone who I believe I can help—even on public transportation. I always carry fliers or postcards about my work or events, and I hand them out or leave some behind—even in restrooms. My events are well attended because I have learned how to promote my work effectively—and this is what you need to learn to do. If you don't truly believe in your work enough to talk about it to everyone, in a positive way, how can you expect others to do so?

The show ended shortly after my last comment. The host thanked us cordially and commented that Author #2 should market himself more. I suggested that he get a publicist to help him, if he could not do it for himself effectively.

Don't Sit and Protest, Get Creative to Turn No to Yes

What's wrong with this picture, sis? Instead of properly using the great marketing opportunity that that popular radio program offered him to inform thousands of listeners about the strong points in his book and his work, Author 2 probably blew it because he was so busy complaining. His approach was self-defeating because he chose to look at the glass as being half empty instead of half full.

He had a somewhat legitimate gripe, but that's life. It gets rough and tough at times, but when it does, you have got to get even tougher and say, "I am not going to let this knock me out." It's okay to fall—we all do at times—but know when to get up, brush off the dirt, and keep moving. You have got to "know your audience." Know how to turn the negative into positive.

Sis, make sure you don't waste precious time complaining when you can use the same energy to find positive ways to improve your situation.

An enterprising and multifaceted sister-friend, Dr. Rosie Milligan, founder of Black Writers on Tour, invented this motto: "Erase *no,* step over *can't,* and move forward with life."

Sis, there will be many times in life when you will get a *no,* but don't let that deter you from pursuing your goals. If you believe in what you are doing, keep pushing ahead. Be bold, but not over-bearing. And never, never, never take rejection personally. A lot of people "who have made it" will not share the truth with you: that their success took a lot of hard work over a long period of time. Some will actually lie and tell you that they were discovered and became an overnight success. Don't fall for the hype.

Don't envy them their success, either. Instead, get working on achieving your own individual goals. Don't get sidetracked by the three self-defeating *C's: competing, copying,* and *comparing.* Success takes a lot of hard work, discipline, focus, and perseverance. Respect others' talents, and don't neglect your own.

IF YOU WANT SUCCESS, PUT FORTH YOUR BEST— AND STICK TO THE TEST

The real truth is that "overnight success" takes an average of five to eight years to accomplish. By the time we hear, see, or read about someone's success, what we are really observing is the result of years of training and preparation. The five-year process is rarely discussed. "Good Choice #4: Turning Stumbling Blocks into Stepping-Stones" will prepare you to get beyond life's barriers.

Your goal should be to become *successful* but not necessarily a *success.* When you aim to be a success, you measure your progress by the outer trappings of the world. You'll always be competing with others to see if you have the "right" car, home, clothes, stocks, country club membership, and so on. But when you aim to be successful, you measure your individual accomplishments by your own standards. It means becoming the best that you can be and enjoying every moment of it, instead of trying to keep up with someone else's definition of success. Whichever road you choose in life, make sure you are the ultimate manager of your own outcome.

Over fifteen years ago, one of my wise uncles and my favorite mentor taught me something that has always stayed with me. He said, "If something is really important to you, do it yourself." At first I thought he was being a bit rigid, but after putting his statement to many tests, voluntarily and involuntarily, throughout the years, I've found that he was absolutely right. Sis, "if something is really important to you, do it yourself."

Have you ever seen the following short story (its author unknown) floating around your office or on the Internet?

> This is a story about people named Everybody, Somebody, Anybody, and Nobody. There was an important job to be done, and Everybody was sure that Somebody would do it. Anybody could have done it, but Nobody did it. Somebody got angry about that, because it was Everybody's job. Everybody thought Anybody could do it. It ended up that Everybody blamed Somebody when Nobody did what Anybody could have done.

"WHEN THE GOING GETS TOUGH, THE TOUGH GET GOING"

In order to get things going in your life, you have to take the initiative. I've heard so many people say "I feel so depressed—if only I could get rid of the clutter in my home," "If only I could shake off the excess fat," or "If only I could finish writing a book." The simple truth is, sis, that the clutter is not going to get up and move itself—*you* have to start throwing away the excess paper, old clothes, and old furnishings. The fat is not going to melt away on its own—*you* have to follow a diet or nutritional plan, and exercise. And the book, will certainly not write itself (trust me)—*you* have to either take pen in hand and start jotting down the words, or start typing away at the keyboard. The point is that to get it done, *you* have to get in motion. Wishing won't make it happen—only action will.

If you notice, most of the people in the Bible who got blessed were already in motion. The Hebrews had to be traveling toward the Red Sea in order for God to part it for them to walk over to the Promised Land. The woman with an issue of blood took the initiative to walk to Jesus and touch his hem in order to be healed. People who were already in motion reaped the reward of a positive outcome.

A brother in Dallas, thirty-five-year-old Stephen, recently got laid off from his firm. His bills were piling up, and he needed a new job right away—the creditors and bill collectors were hounding him day and night. Panicking, he called me for advice and some words of comfort.

I told him not to panic but to have faith, because God always helps people who are in motion. I told him to put the word out to everyone he knew, scope the papers, and set up a few interviews for that week. Then he was to call me, and we would pray together.

After he set up the interviews, he called. The job he really wanted, he said, required that he bring a list of four references. He already had two and asked if he could use me as a third. I had known him for over a year, so I said yes. The interview was scheduled for the next afternoon, and he was a bit nervous because he didn't have the fourth required reference.

STOP FRETTING AND START GETTING YOUR SHARE OF SUCCESS

I told him not to worry, "but let us pray." We did. If the job he really wanted was for him, I said, he would have it. If it not, then he would get a better one—but he would have to go into the interview believing.

"Even without enough references?" he asked.

"Oh, yes," I confirmed. "You just get going and do your part, and God will do His."

I did not hear from him for three or four days. Then he called with a happy-sounding voice to say, "You know, your theory about being in motion really works. I went in with faith, did the interview, went home, and gave God thanks in advance, as you suggested. The same afternoon, the woman and her assistant who interviewed me called to tell me I got the job. And here's the surprise—they didn't even bother to check my references. They were so impressed with my résumé and background that they offered me a nice salary with good benefits. This is great! Thank you."

You are quite welcome, my brother. Give God the glory.

"A Rolling Stone Gathers No Moss"

Thirty-nine-year-old Diane went through a similar ordeal. She was laid off and was looking for gainful employment, but six months later she was still collecting unemployment checks. She still had two months' worth of checks to collect, when she received a letter from the unemployment office stating that her next check would be her last, and that she would not be able to file for benefits again until a few months had passed.

She called me that same afternoon, seeking advice. She had no emergency money put aside. Her rent was due in two weeks, and her car payment and utility and phone bills in three. The aviation school to which she had applied had just accepted her, and she had to pay an admission fee of two hundred dollars right away. "I don't know what I'm going to do. This must be a test from God to see if I am a true believer or something." Her voice trembled with worry.

"If it is a test, then make sure you pass by hanging on to your belief," I insisted. "God has a way of shining through even in the darkest hour. It may sometimes seem as if He's an eleventh-hour

God, but He always comes through. Don't worry," I comforted. "Set up interviews right away, even if they're only with temp agencies. If you take the first step, God will guide your feet through. If you really want to go to that school, pray on it, and ask God if you should pay for it out of your unemployment check. I'll pray for you tonight. When you go to your interviews, make sure you go in with the belief that 'you can do all things through Christ in you.'"

Diane called me the very next day to say that she had prayed and had "a strong urge" to pay the school's admission fee. "If this is what your mind, heart, and spirit are telling you to do, then go for it," I said. She did.

Two days later, Diane called to say, "You won't believe what happened. I went to the aviation school and paid my admission fee. Something told me to look on the students' message board. They had job postings there. I copied three that I was interested in. I interviewed for one yesterday morning, and another in the afternoon—and I got offered both!" She was elated as she continued, "They need someone to start right away. Today I went on the third interview, just to see how it compared with the other two. It's okay, but the position doesn't open for two months. Anyway, I accepted the first one, and I start tomorrow morning."

SOMETIMES YOU'VE GOT TO PUT THE CART BEFORE THE HORSE

Sis, God truly works in mysterious ways. In June 1991, I decided to write and self-publish my first book, *The Fortune of Being Yourself.* I didn't know anything about writing a book, much less about publishing one. All I knew was that I was leading my holistic image-consultant workshops and seminars in America, the Caribbean, and Europe—and people kept asking me to write a book so they could have "a part of me to take home with them." So I decided to go for it.

I told Tina, one of my closest friends at the time, that I was going to finance a book project from scratch and make it a best-seller within a year. She looked at me puzzled and out of concern asked, "How are you going to do that by yourself? Do you know anything about the book industry?"

"Nope!" I declared courageously. "But I'm about to learn. I won't be doing this alone, because in the Book of Matthew, Jesus says that if God takes care of the birds in air and the grass of the fields, he will take care of me, too, if I will only believe. And I do believe with my entire being, and I am ready to do the work to get this book done."

My bold statement shocked Tina—the look on her face told me that she thought I'd gone out on a limb. Although she and I were close friends, we had never discussed spirituality in depth. Tina believes the Bible is a beautiful book of fiction. I *know* it is real and that it is God's personal letter to all who will believe. Clearly, we had our different opinions, but, we were good friends and respected each other's boundaries. She never challenged my belief, and I never challenged her disbelief.

But when she kept asking, "How are you going to do this book project from scratch?" I had to answer truthfully. "I don't know exactly how I'm going to do it yet," I admitted. "It will be revealed to me as I go along, and I will do the necessary work. God has always guided me through. As sure as He lives, I don't know how it will be done, but because He lives, I do know that it will be done."

"Wow," Tina uttered in disbelief. "Good luck."

FINE-TUNE YOUR FAITH, PLAN YOUR PROMOTION, AND GET INTO MOTION

After that conversation, I got busy. Praying for guidance, I rolled up my sleeves, went to Barnes and Noble, and got my hands on every book on self-publishing, publicity, promotion, and marketing that I could find. It got rough many times, but I did not waver. I kept focused, used the information that was helpful, and disregarded that which wasn't. I spent many sleepless nights typing the manuscript and planning the publicity. Whenever I felt my energy level running low (and there were many times), I prayed, "Father, please lend me a helping hand, and refuel my body temple." It worked.

WHEN YOU'VE PAID YOUR TUITION, YOU'LL ENJOY LIFE'S FRUITION

A year later, *The Fortune of Being Yourself* was in its second printing, and I sold the rights for the Spanish translation to Panarama Editorial in Mexico. At one of my book-signings, Tina confided in me, "Last year when you told me you were going to do this, I did not believe you. I knew you were creative, but I said to myself that there was no way you could pull this off in such a short period of time, and by yourself. You proved me wrong. I apologize. I am so proud of you."

"Thanks. You don't have to apologize. You just have to believe. You'd be surprised how powerfully and mysteriously God moves," I said. "With God all things are possible."

"I sometimes want to believe, but it's so hard because I need someone real in front of me," confided Tina. "I guess it's from my upbringing. I'm not an idealist, I'm a realist. I need to see the actual proof before I can believe. How do you keep your faith in a God you've never seen? How do you know He really exists?

"Do you believe your thoughts are real?" I asked.

"Of course," she answered.

"Have you ever seen your thoughts?"

"No."

"Then how do you know they're real?"

SEEING IS BELIEVING, BUT BELIEVING BEFORE SEEING IS A LEAP INTO GLORY

Tina paused for a brief moment before answering. "Because I feel them," she said. "Of course you do," I continued. "You also have never seen the wind, but you know it exists, because you feel it. It's the same thing with God, who is the Creator of your thoughts, the wind, and you. All you have to do is open your mind and heart to feel His presence all around you, inside of you, and to see it through the manifestation of the people, places, and things around you.

"At the end of the Book of John, after Jesus was resurrected, He appeared to His disciples, but Thomas, was not present. When the other disciples told Thomas that Jesus was alive, he said he would have to see and touch Him to believe. Eight days later, when Jesus appeared before Thomas, He told him to touch Him since he needed proof to restore his faith.

"Thomas finally believed. Jesus said, 'Thomas, because you have seen me, you believe, but blessed are they that have not seen, and still believe.'

"It's a personal relationship that you have to develop with God by accepting and believing that He exists, but if you don't believe, you won't be able to see a lot 'blessings in disguise' in your life. God is not a person, but He is very personal. He is a constant source of guidance, love, and companionship. All you have to do is be at ease and ask Him to manifest Himself in your body temple, mind, and spirit."

USE IT OR LOSE IT

My "guardian angel" mother, Aunt D, who is truly a blessing in my life, shared this story with me. You may have heard it before—it's about a minister and a soap-maker:

One day both men were having a conversation about their chosen professions. They were walking down a crowded street, and they saw two people arguing and cursing each other. The soap-maker turned to the minister and asked, "Do you honestly believe the spirituality you preach really cleans and cleanses people?"

"Most definitely," answered the minister.

"If it's as good as you say," asked the soap-maker, "then why are there so many unclean people in the world?"

"Let me think for a few minutes," said the minister. "I'll answer you in a little while."

They walked a few more blocks and saw two panhandlers covered in dirt and begging for spare change. The minister gave them some coins, then turned to the soap-maker and asked, "Do you honestly believe the soap you make really cleans and cleanses people?"

"Why, of course," confirmed the soap-maker.

"If it's as good as you say," asked the minister, "then why are there so many unclean people in the world?"

"Well," answered the soap-maker in a smug tone, "people have to use it for it to work for them."

"Exactly," concluded the minister. "You have rightfully answered both of our questions."

The moral of the story: You have to put in your share, so God can exercise His share and guide you. It's a partnership. God will demonstrate many blessings in your life, but *you* have to initiate the process and use your faith. Plan effectively, and be willing to do the work. With God you can never lose.

PLAN YOUR PURPOSE IN LIFE

Many people spend their lives wishing to achieve their dreams but failing to properly plan how to do it or carry out the plan. They drift aimlessly along, taking each day as it comes, accepting what is dished out to them. They make no plans for living. They have not decided what their purpose in life is. They merely wish to do better, or to be in better surroundings. Most common of all: "I wish I had a million dollars."

You cannot wish yourself into having an ideal relationship or a better body. You can, however, create goals, make plans and get to work on them. Write down what you expect to achieve, and ask

God to guide you in each step on your path. The time to start is now.

> My personal plan for the next month is . . .
>> Three months . . .
>> Six months . . .
> My personal plan for the next year is . . .
>> Three years . . .
>> Five years . . .
>> Ten years . . .
> My personal plan for life is . . .

WHEN OPPORTUNITY KNOCKS, ANSWER THE DOOR

I want to conclude this chapter by emphasizing taking calculated chances. Have you heard the story of the man caught in a flash flood? He was a very religious man and was positive that God would rescue him. He struggled to climb to the roof of his house, where he waited for God to save him. As the water rose higher, a man in a tugboat rowed by and offered to rescue him. The stranded man graciously refused, saying, "Thanks for your offer, but God will save me."

About two hours later, the water rose above the second floor. Another boater came by in a motorboat and offered the man a seat. "No thanks," he declined again with unshakable faith. "I'm waiting on God to save me."

Three hours later, he was clinging to the roof as the out-of-control water rose and wrapped itself around his ankles. Instantly, a helicopter dropped him a ladder, but he refused the help because he was convinced that God was testing his faith. About an hour later, the raging current of the floodwaters washed him away, and he drowned.

As his soul approached the gateway to Heaven, he demanded an immediate explanation from the archangel on duty. "I kept believing and praying. Why didn't you save me?" he admonished.

Sternly, the archangel replied, "Oh, we tried, we tried, we tried! We sent you a tugboat, a motorboat, and a helicopter!"

Sis, don't miss your blessing. Don't take idle chances by waiting to be rescued. Choose to be an initiator—take calculated chances. Make concrete plans for living, ask God for guidance, and get in motion.

good choice

#8

Giving Stress a Perpetual Rest

Let not your heart be troubled,
neither let it be afraid.
John 14:27

Statistics from the American Heart Association state that black women in the United States are *three to five times more likely* to die or to suffer from cardiovascular disease than are white women. Isn't this alarming?

Mental and emotional stresses are two major contributors to cardiovascular disease. And two of the major contributors to the mental and emotional stresses that black women face in America are racism and sexism.

As a matter of fact, I've yet to meet a sister who has never experienced some form of racism and sexism in her life. Let me share two personal experiences of my own.

When I first graduated from college, I was employed as a retail executive in the World Trade Center. I usually wore well-tailored business suits or dresses, kept myself well groomed, and wore my hair in a shoulder-length bob. One particular afternoon, I was returning to my office from lunch, eyes focused straight ahead—and anyone who has ever walked in New York City (and especially in the World Trade Center) during the lunch hour knows that you have to keep your attention focused straight ahead in order to make your way through the massive crowd in one piece.

So there I was, minding my own business, in stride with the crowd, when suddenly someone tugged my hair from behind and uttered rudely, "You trying to act white." I was so baffled and shocked that I was speechless. I was even more distraught to turn around and discover that it was a black man, early twenties, casually dressed, who had executed this disturbing behavior.

Now, I have always tried to display warmth and respect to all human beings, and to give an extra dose of compassion to my brothers and sisters. But I could not believe what this brother had done. I was hurt and angry at the same time. My temper flared, and my stress level rose, but I refused to align myself with his mean-spirited behavior. So I just shook my head with disappointment and walked away from him.

I would like to know what made him think he was entitled to throw his ridiculous insult at me or even touch me in any way. I bet he wouldn't have done that to a man. His sexist behavior was deplorable.

As if that weren't bad enough, several months later I was standing at an intersection waiting for the traffic light to turn to green, when a white male, early thirties, business attire, whispered in my ear, "Hello, brown sugar. I would like to have you. I love my women like I like my coffee, hot and black." His racist utterance had my stomach in knots. How dare he disrespect me in that way? I was so angry that I looked at him with total disgust and told him, "Oh, go to hell, you idiot."

RACISM AND SEXISM ARE MAJOR STRESS FACTORS FOR SISTERS

Incidents like these two are nothing new to black women. Many sisters face both racism and sexism on a daily basis—in the workplace, in relationships, and in social settings. Black women are especially stressed out because they are burdened with negative images and false standards, and they have had to keep their mouths shut about their pain for far too long. And whenever we do speak up about unfair treatment, we are stereotyped in society (and in our own race) as "loud and aggressive," while our white sisters who voice their gripes are labeled "independent and assertive." What a difference—is this nonsense or what?

GETTING BEYOND THE PAIN

Sis, don't run your life based on anyone's opinions and stereotypes. It is very important for you to redefine your life by your own standards. Follow all the good choices in this book, and become a lovely and magnificent woman of color. Make it a habit to tune out the daily chaos and create peace within your own mind and body with the relaxation, visualization, and affirmation techniques in "Good Choice # 4: Turning Stumbling Blocks into Stepping-Stones." And when you feel like speaking up, by all means do so in a thorough and polite, yet straightforward and firm manner—don't hold on to pain.

The stimulus of pain causes a response of stress in your body temple, and it invades your organs, nerves, and cell tissues. Speak up, sis, and if someone, anyone, or everyone doesn't like it—well, too bad for them. It's time for black women to stop suffering from those heart attacks, ulcers, migraines, and high blood pressure—all linked to high levels of stress.

Being disrespected, taken for granted, overworked, underpaid, or mistreated in any way stresses both your emotional and your physical immune systems. Here are some telltale signs of stress: Your heart rate increases, you feel a gripping feeling in your stomach, your muscles tense, you perspire more, and your blood pressure increases.

A *Fact* of Life Doesn't Have to Be a *Way* of Life

Sis, there are many things in life that you won't be able to control, like people's behavior, weather conditions, and aging. But you can control your reactions to them and manage your stress level accordingly. Stress may be a *fact* of life, sis, but it doesn't have to be a *way* of life.

Let's take a look at how to effectively control stress. There are two types of stress—positive and negative.

Positive stress is a short-term heightened response to the necessity of meeting a certain challenge, deadline, or project. It can help you to focus, concentrate, and reach peak performance. In fact, most people bring forth their best creative work under such pressure. Then, after the project has been completed, or the deadline or challenge met, they sit back, relax, and enjoy the fruits of their labor. This relaxation period rids the body of stress and helps them to accumulate the emotional, spiritual, and physical reserves to face the next project or challenge. This kind of stress is healthy.

Negative stress is a long-term, lingering response to challenges, people's behavior, or fear. After you meet a confrontation or a challenge, you stay revved up and don't, won't, or can't relax. With no relaxation period between challenges, emotional and physical strain can be the outcome. Your body may react with clenched teeth, tensed muscles, headaches, upset stomach, clammy hands, or a nervous twitch. This is the type of ongoing stress that has been associated with heart attacks, strokes, and high blood pressure. It is unhealthy.

How to Move from Stress Victim to Stress Victor

In order to manage your stress effectively, you first have to pinpoint the situations that make you feel tense. These could include work overload, minor irritations, major lifestyle changes, or a combination of all. Drinking alcohol, smoking, and using drugs do not eliminate or relieve stress. Once you've identified the problems that make you feel uneasy, angry, or miserable, you must make adjustments to ease the tension. For instance:

WORK OVERLOAD

Work overload can surface when you are being pulled in many directions at the same time, either at home or in the workplace. What with the children, bills, mate, and household chores, things may seem unbearable, unmanageable, or out of control at times. At work, you may face pressure to perform, incomplete projects, or a disgruntled boss or coworkers, and you may feel there are just not enough hours in the day to do everything that's required of you.

Solution. Taking a quick break to sit down, relax, and breathe deeply will do wonders. Realize that you won't be able to solve everything at once. Take one minute out of every hour to do nothing but breathe. Sometimes just moving a short distance away from your challenges can help you find creative ways to handle them. You'll be surprised how just sixty seconds of relaxation can calm and refresh you. Figure out what should be done immediately, what can wait until later, and what can be done the next day. Take it one hour at a time.

MINOR IRRITATIONS

Minor irritations are the dreary little day-to-day events that annoy you. Lost keys, traffic jams, petty arguments, missed buses, and misplaced telephone books are hardly mind-blowing activities, but they can build up and cause side effects. Some of these little hassles can cause emotional and physical health-related complications, so be alert to the incidents that increase your temper, blood pressure, and heart rate.

Solution. Avoiding irritations can help get rid of the little hassles that accumulate and become negative stress. If traffic jams and the rush-hour commute "drive you crazy," then get together with friends and start (or join) a carpool. This will definitely cut back on gridlock. Why not try taking public transportation on some days? If you feel rushed, annoyed, or anxious about not getting to work on time, try getting to bed an hour earlier at night, and getting up an hour earlier in the morning. Pace yourself effectively.

MAJOR LIFESTYLE CHANGES

Major lifestyle changes, whether positive or negative, can have an overwhelming effect on your life. A positive event like planning a wedding, the birth of a baby, buying a new home, or getting a promotion, can cause as much stress as a negative event like going through a divorce, experiencing the death of a loved one, losing your home, or being downsized from your job. Major events cause you to take on many new, different, and unknown situations. Adapting to major changes can be stressful in itself.

Solution. Having a support system in place will help you to stay grounded during major changes. Surround yourself with friends, family, coworkers, associates, support groups, or health professionals to whom you can air your feelings and concerns. Whenever you experience a lifestyle change, make an effort to keep the other aspects of your life functioning as usual. For instance, if you've started a new career, bought a new home, or become a new parent, try your best to keep doing the little things that bring you joy. And above all, talk to friends. Knowing that you're not alone during major lifestyle changes is a great comfort.

SIS, YOU'VE GOT TO HURRY AND GET RID OF WORRY

If you stop to think about it, you'll realize that the main cause of negative stress is *worry*. We worry about being unable to pay the bills or meet a deadline. We worry about disliking our jobs or about pacing ourselves improperly. We worry about getting fired, getting sick, getting evicted; we worry about being late, being lonely, being ridiculed, not being liked, or not fitting into certain social circles.

Many different worries prevent people from being happy. They worry about their families, and their looks, their relationships. Black women especially worry about everything from what other people think of them to the texture of their hair.

A verse in the Bible cautions us about worry. Matthew 13:23 says, "He also that received seed among the thorns is he that heareth the word, [but] the care of the world choke the word and he become unfruitful."

Here is my interpretation of this wise proverb. The word is "peace, be still, and let God be your guide," sis. If you hear and believe this "word," then you will receive blessings even against all odds. But worry about other people's expectations and opinions will cut off your peace of mind, and you will not accomplish much.

On that note, sis, let's get rid of worry.

BREATHE YOUR WORRIES AWAY

Worrying is unproductive and unhealthy. The more you worry, the worse things become; the worse things become, the more you stress your physical and psychological immune systems. Instead of worrying, breathe deeply. This will help to calm your system so that you can think of creative ways to deal with your situation.

Try this deep breathing technique, and you'll see how it helps to relax your mind and body:

1. Stand up straight with both arms relaxed at your side.
2. Inhale slowly through your nostrils. Feel the air filling your diaphragm and solar plexus. As you breathe in, slowly raise both arms from your sides, palms facing upward. (Inhale the positive.)
3. Bring both hands directly over your head, let your palms kiss each other, and hold it for a count of six.

4. Then slowly exhale through your mouth. Feel the air being released from your center. As you breathe out, slowly lower both arms to your sides, palms facing downward. (Let out the negative.)

5. Repeat this exercise four to six times.

MEET IT, GREET IT, AND DEFEAT IT

Worry disappears when you apply positive action. If you are worried about your job performance, concentrate on doing constructive tasks at work. Aim for more productivity, or take more interest in your work. If you are worried about becoming sick, safeguard your health: Eat healthy, exercise, get mammograms, have your blood pressure checked often, and be spiritually at ease in your own body temple.

Sis, get into the habit of replacing negative thoughts with positive ones. Continually repeat, "I feel well and perfectly healthy." If you are worried about a loved one who is far away, a simple phone call can be very reassuring.

Whatever your worry, take positive steps to overcome it. Tell yourself, "I am going to *meet it, greet it,* and *defeat it.*" First you *meet* the worry by recognizing that it exists; next you *greet* it by realizing you have to get rid of it; then you *defeat* it by taking positive action.

One of the most effective ways I've found to combat worrisome stress is to ask yourself, "What is the worst thing that can happen if I don't get what I'm aiming for?" Once you have asked the question out loud without fear, answer it. Then boldly ask yourself, "If that happens, what would I do next?" Answer yourself again, then ask, "What would I do after that?" Keep inquiring until you find a solution to the challenge you face.

This practice will put your mind at ease. Once it becomes a general practice, you'll find yourself being less worried, more productive, and happier. As a matter of fact, sis, strive for happiness. Stress and happiness cannot exist at the same time. If you have a happy outlook and a happy spirit, you *will not* and *cannot* have a stressed-out body or a stressful mind.

HAPPINESS IS FREE

When you ask most people, "What would make you happy?" the most common reply is "I would be happy if I had more money."

Money is important, but it cannot buy happiness. *Happiness is free.* The amount of time and energy people spend trying to get happy would be better spent just *being* happy.

The stories of two sisters prove that happiness is self-determined, not dollar-determined.

Several years ago, while engaged in a promotion for a leading cosmetics company, I had the pleasure of working with a very special individual, Elizabeth A., who is now a very good friend of mine.

Liz, as I call her, was always pleasant and cheerful, even under the most trying circumstances. She worked well under pressure. She stayed calm. Anyone who came into contact with her was affected by her cheerfulness.

One afternoon while talking about life in general, I asked her, "Liz, you always seem so pleasant and happy. I think that's wonderful. How do you stay so sunny?"

"Well, Grace," she answered, "I like myself, and I enjoy people. I like being alive—and I'm thankful for it. Each day of my life is a gift. I appreciate it and live it to the best of my ability."

Life isn't any easier for Liz than it is for other people. She is a single mother with three children. She worked her way through graduate school while caring for her own mother as well as her children. In addition to being a teacher, she has to work part time in order to make ends meet. Liz tells me this with much joy. *She loves her life and does the best with what she has.* She has found the key to happiness.

THE NEED TO IMPRESS CREATES A TERRIBLE MESS

Another friend of mine, whom I also met several years ago, has a different story. I'll call her Jenny M.

Jenny seems to be the woman who has it all. She comes from a very affluent family. She is employed as an executive vice president in a major advertising agency. Her husband is on the board of directors for a prestigious merchandising corporation. They have two children, and own three apartments on Manhattan's sophisticated East Side—one of which is a glorious penthouse. They have a country home in Westchester, a summer home in the Hamptons, property in the Caribbean, three impressive cars, and a well-padded portfolio of stocks and bonds, to name just a few of their assets. These folks are superwealthy.

If money could buy happiness, Jenny should be one of the happiest women on the planet. She is not. She loves her children, but she hardly spends any time with them because she is so deeply involved with her work. She avoids being home with a husband whom she does not like very much. Both husband and wife secretly indulge in extramarital affairs.

"Jenny," I asked one afternoon, "if you are both so unhappy and have lost respect for each other, why don't you see a marriage counselor?" I must say, her answer was a sad one indeed.

"It's way past that stage. I can't divorce Erwin until I find a potential second husband. My parents think he is ideal for me. They are very close. I don't know how to explain it to them. There would be so much gossip at the country club. How could I stand that?

This situation has been going on for over five years. Jenny, to this day, is miserable, is stuck in an unhappy marriage, and is still seeking happiness.

GET INTO THE HAPPINESS HABIT

Your life is too precious to be wasted in negative environments. Every day find at least six things that make you happy. Make a list of them as you move through your day. At night, before you go to bed, meditate on those six things. Over time, this process will become a vital part of your personality. Reviewing your personal happy list right before falling asleep will give you pleasant dreams instead of nightmares.

Here is an example of a happy list:

1. I feel happy because I am living to experience the new millennium.
2. I feel happy because I have a job, an opportunity to earn an income.
3. I feel happy because I had a chance to cheer someone up today.
4. I feel happy because I am meeting new people every day.
5. I feel happy because I am healthy.
6. I feel happy because God woke me up this morning.

Abraham Lincoln once said, "Most people are about as happy as they make up their minds to be." Sis, this is your time now. Choose to be as happy as *you* want to be. Don't let anyone rain on your parade, and give stress a permanent rest.

good choice

#9

Rewriting Your Life's Script

Behold old things are passed away, all things are become new.
II Corinthians 5:17

Life is a gigantic theater, and we are actors playing our various roles. At birth, we were handed a script prepared by a self-appointed playwright. Throughout our life experience, we have had to enact many unsuitable and unhappy scenes.

But nowhere in our individual scripts is it written that the script cannot be changed. The truth is that we can rewrite our script and redirect our own performance at any time we desire. This is the "truth that will set you free." We each have the ability to dismiss old beliefs, create new scenes, and cast new characters.

We are able to do this with the most valuable gift we possess— our minds. This precious gift from our Divine Creator, *free will,* is always available to serve us, making us cocreators with God.

Jesus tried hard to make this truth visible to us each time He stated, "Be it done to you according to your faith." The underlying message is "I do not change your life or heal you by myself. Your *faith* and *belief* that I can do so is what allows me to perform miracles in your life." He could easily do it on His own, of course, but He wants us to exercise our God-given gift of faith.

You Are the Producer of Your Own Life's Drama— Why Not Put on a Masterpiece Production?

God has given us the go-ahead to clean, cleanse, and strengthen our lives. But spiritually sluggish human beings keep ignoring this blessed gift. Benjamin Franklin said it best: "God helps those who help themselves." Instead of looking to professed psychics, and fortune-tellers, turn to the greatest guide of all—your free will—and believe so that you can receive and achieve.

As black women in America, other people have set various standards regarding our characteristics, features, complexions, and thinking. But these superficial standards can have no personal effect on us, unless we ourselves choose to believe in or accept them.

Our minds are the only possessions over which we have total control. If we make conscious efforts to refuse the opinions of others, they cannot be absorbed into our thinking. Your mind is your own personal safe-deposit box. Only you possess the key to either open or close it, and to decide which thoughts to put in or take out.

All humans strive to reach a state of contentment, but few succeed because most look for satisfaction in other people, places, and things. Outside escapes may supply temporary joy, but they have no lasting influence. True contentment can come only from within, where we can learn to become at peace with ourselves.

Why Waste Another Day in Misery?

Too many sisters of color have been slipping through life, unable to claim their birthright, unable to ignite the sparks of true joy. As black women today, we have a golden opportunity to take heed and create our own personalized productions. We can start at this very moment.

The following is a sample script in which you actually write your own program for an enjoyable life. It is designed to serve as a guideline for your journey toward empowerment, achievement, and peace of mind

EMPOWERING MYSELF

PLAYWRIGHT: _____
(your name)

Act I, Scene 1
NURTURING THE INTERIOR CHILD

Our personalities are formed by the situations, events, and teachings we have accumulated during our life span. Although we can alter our thinking and improve ourselves at any point we choose, the foundation of our true selves was already formed by the age of ten. All other traits were later added to our primary bases, building these complicated structures that we now know as our *selves.*

In order to find out more about our true selves and to rid ourselves of disharmonious programming, we must look within. We must contact and nuture the little stranger whom we have hidden deep inside—*the interior child,* the child who is lonely, lost, and longing to be loved.

The way we handle situations depends on how we were treated as children. For example, if we were taught to speak only when we were spoken to, we become apprehensive of expressing our opinions and fearful of letting others know when we are uncomfortable.

If we have been told that we will never amount to much, we have become very subservient to other people's needs, many times neglecting our own. Any extremity is unhealthy for our well-being. If we were overindulged, with our every demand catered to, we grew up expecting the world to revolve around us, and we are truly hurt when others do not meet our expectations.

Traumatic experiences can cause us to retreat within, cutting off very important parts of ourselves from life. We will subconsciously act out our unpleasant memories because they were not corrected, just pushed aside and hidden.

Most people take Socrates' admonition "Know thyself" to mean "Know thy conscious or exterior self," without any regard for the interior self, the true self, which is hidden deep within, waiting to be nurtured.

Let's take time to know the interior self, beginning with the experiences of the little child you once were and still are within. We must *face, erase, replace,* and *embrace* your unhealthy memories.

This scene is designed to help you rid yourself of negative beliefs and insecurities caused by childhood experiences. Thoughts and feelings that stem from them may be presently causing disharmony among your mind, body, and spirit. Any deep cleansing, like this one, always causes tears and pain. But the tears wash away the old to make room for the new, while pain is not unhealthy but truthful.

Any unpleasant thing that happened to you as a child was not your fault. You should not be held responsible for any of these unfortunate experiences, nor blame yourself for them. Contentment will begin when you have spanned a bridge of positive memories between your childhood and adulthood. This will create a happy, wholesome self.

I NOW FACE IT

Write the story of your childhood—where you were born, the environment in which you were brought up, your family, home, school, and so on. Write down specific experiences that you remember that caused you to feel frightened, upset, angry, hated, alone, or embarrassed.

I NOW ERASE IT

Review your story of the little *you.* Find photos of yourself if possible. Study them carefully. Talk to that child. Find out how she is feeling. What makes her afraid? How can you help her? Comfort her; hug her. Let her know that you love her and that she will never be alone again.

Tell her not to be afraid, not to believe any cruel or untrue thing that anyone may be saying about her. Let her know that she can trust you, that you were sent to guide her—that you will protect her and make sure that no one can ever hurt her again.

I NOW REPLACE IT

Relax, and visualize that child being comforted by someone who cares for and loves her. Help her to create a happy childhood. Believe and accept that you have the ability to do so. Share the power of positive affirmations with your interior child. Help her to rewrite her story. This time record only the good, positive images and experiences about this precious little girl. Make sure you emphasize how happy she is.

I NOW EMBRACE IT

Take a look in a mirror—just stare and look deep into your eyes (the windows to your soul), and tell yourself, "God loves me. This is a new me. I am valuable. I do love me. Thank you, God, for making me."

At first it may seem uncomfortable to stare into your own eyes, but keep doing it until you become at ease, and enjoy your own reflection.

Act I, Scene 2
DESIGNING MY PERSONAL PROFILE

Write a detailed description of your basic mannerisms and preferences. For example, write about your favorite color and the way you dress; the types of books and music you like; the places, hobbies, pets, movies, or topics you enjoy.

The things I like most about myself are . . .
The things I dislike most about myself are . . .
I could correct these things if . . .

My affirmations to improve the way I feel about myself:

I am original, unique and special. I am one of a kind; therefore, I am priceless.

I am now at peace with myself. I am confident, courageous, successful, and bold.

(continue to create your own affirmations)

Act I, Scene 3
ACCENTUATING MY BEAUTIFUL ASSETS

This scene allows you to develop a special admiration for your own beauty. Write down at least six compliments for each of the following features. Don't be modest! As a matter of fact, let your ego have fun emphasizing your beautiful assets.

SKIN	HAIR	NOSE	LIPS
SMILE	TEETH	EYES	NAILS
HANDS	FEET	BODY	HEIGHT
WEIGHT	POSTURE		

Act II, Scene 1
FREEING MYSELF OF NEGATIVE COMPANY

One of the most emotionally draining situations we may experience is lack of support from loved ones—be they family members, friends, or lovers. We all grow at different paces in life. When you've accelerated past or outgrown a certain level of thinking, even some of the closest people in your life may have difficulty understanding or accepting this. They may unintentionally hold you back by discouraging your dreams. At times, they may do and say belittling things that cause you emotional hurt, confusion, and insecurity.

The sad truth is that when faced with disapproval from a loved one, most people give up their innermost dreams. They abandon their hopes of flying to the heights of success and instead flutter in mediocrity, all because of bad advice.

Their loved ones may genuinely mean well but are afraid of being left behind. But others, unfortunately, are simply envious and selfish. Accepting advice from people who don't understand you is like taking a beautifully designed couture dress to be altered by a five-and-dime seamstress. You are too important to be tailored by a five-and-dime adviser.

Sis, you must be true to yourself. Respect your own feelings. Firmly but politely assure these people that you do love them and will always be there for them. But they will have to respect the fact that *you* know what is best for you.

Explain that you are no longer a baby bird hanging out in a self-contained nest, that you are becoming an enchanting bird of paradise and are ready to spread your wings. Let them know that it would make you happy if they would come fly with you, but you will no longer be enclosed.

Make a list of all the people who cause you discomfort, and the reasons why. After you've compiled your list, review and discuss it with them. Let them know how much this affects you, and really try to work things out.

But if they are still unwilling to grant you the respect you deserve, don't react negatively. Instead, realize this plain truth: *You can't change others, but you can certainly change yourself.*

Remain focused on your goals. Don't compromise. You can continue to be polite, loving, and friendly, but do not share your dreams with them; just move out of their reach.

My affirmations for freeing myself of negative company:

It is unfortunate that ___ does not understand my desires. I love him/her anyway, but I have to move on.

I know that ___ loves and means me well, but I have to be true to my dreams, and I hope that he/she will grow to understand me someday.

Although ___ has hurt me, I hold no anger toward him/her. I forgive him/her and wish him/her well in his/her circle.

I now choose friends and associates who respect my thinking, who I can exchange stimulating ideas with, and who enhance my growth.

(continue to create your own affirmations)

Act II, Scene 2
LABORING WITH LOVE

Write a description of your perfect day at work. Create a scene that is ideal for you. Observe and record your surroundings, your expressions, and your feelings. What are you doing, what are you wearing, and who are you interacting with? Are things running smoothly? Take into consideration the following points when describing your ideal labor of love:

1. Why do I like it?
2. What do I need from it?
3. What do I want from it?
4. How can I help others by it?
5. How can it make me a better person?
6. I have been unable to pursue my ideal career because . . .
7. The skills I need to be qualified for this work are . . .
8. I can obtain these skills if . . .
9. The skills I already have that qualify me for this work are . . .
10. I now choose to pursue my ideal career in the following ways . . .

Act III, Scene 1
CREATING MY PERFECT LIFESTYLE
Write a short story describing the ideal life you want for yourself. Write in the present tense; be specific. Live it as you record it. Let your imagination run wild. Don't limit yourself to what you think may or may not be possible. Become uninhibited, and walk through it with total freedom.

Use the following three categories to assist you: people, places, and things.

People—Whom do you socialize with, work with, have fun with, or travel with? What types of people are part of your surroundings— actors, authors, athletes; bankers, bakers, businessmen? What are the different age groups? What are the ethnic, social, political, educational, economic, or religious backgrounds?

Places—Where do you live? In a Hollywood mansion, a New York penthouse, a London flat, a Swiss chalet, a Caribbean beach house, a Texas farm, or a simple, cozy country home? Where do you vacation, work, shop, dine, relax? Which continents, countries, or islands? Which hotels, resorts, boutiques, stores, or restaurants?

Things—What do you own? Stocks, bonds, clothing, jewelry, cars, yachts, planes, art, pets? What do you like to do? What kind of work, hobbies, entertainment, and recreations do you have? Do you dance, design, or discover? Are you a secretary, a scientist, or a sculptor?

As you create your ideal lifestyle, remember not to hinder your thoughts in any way. Write as if you had all the freedom, money, power, and skills necessary to live your incredible fantasy.

After you have finished composing your soul-searching short story, you'll realize that some of the people, places, and things you've written about may be more meaningful than others. The next part of this scene will help you define the top priorities for achieving your desired lifestyle.

Arrange your fantasy into three divisions as follows:

Division 1: I must have
Division 2: I want, but don't really need
Division 3: I can actually do without

By breaking down your desires, you will gain a clearer picture of your indispensable ones. Create a concrete plan of action for obtaining the elements in Division 1. By getting focused, you will be able to direct your creative energies toward turning your fantasy into reality.

Act III, Scene 2
LIVING MY LIFE TO THE FULLEST TODAY

People have very little respect for time. But death is something natural that we all must eventually face. People don't like to discuss this, and that's understandable. Still, it is as important a characteristic of nature as birth is. Unfortunately, most of the thousands of people who will die today never truly enjoyed the voyage.

Sis, at this point, you have the opportunity to take charge of your life. Just for this moment, pretend that this is your last day on Earth, and you want to enjoy each moment to the fullest. Write a description of how you would spend this important day. Who would you get in touch with? A long-lost friend perhaps, or maybe you would make amends with someone for a misunderstanding. What activities would you enjoy? How would you pamper yourself? Is there someone you like to say thank you to but have not bothered to do so?

If today were my last day on Earth, I would . . .

When you have completed writing your plan for living today, review your list and select the things that you can actually do for yourself today. Do them. Sis, your life is too important to put off till tomorrow what can make you happy today.

Epilogue

Weeping may endure for a night, but joy cometh in the morning.
Thou hast turned for me my mourning into dancing: thou hast put off my
sackcloth, and girded me with gladness.
And in my prosperity I said, I shall not be moved.
PSALM 30

good choice

#10

Using Your "Praying Energy" for "Staying Energy"

And all things, whatsoever ye ask in prayer, believing,
ye shall receive.

Matthew 21:22

Let's face facts. Life can get frustrating at times—*extremely* frustrating. People get frustrated over parking spaces, traffic jams, cable bills, furniture delivery dates, wedding planning, and hairstyle selection, to name just a few.

In all my years of research and application, both in the classroom and in the real world, I have found that the most effective way to combat frustration is through some good old-fashioned prayer. The type of prayer that our grandmothers and great-grandmothers did—those were some seriously spiritual women in the olden days.

I have had two strong praying role models in my life. One was my grandmother, Edwina Hunt, my father's mother, a white Jamaican of British descent with a black woman's soul. Granny, as I affectionately called her, certainly had a sister's soul. Nobody could pray like Granny. My natural mother went to Europe to pursue her modeling career, and for the first eight years of my life in Jamaica, Granny and Aunt D (my guardian mother and Granny's niece) raised my sister Angie and me.

Granny prayed about everything. When she lifted up her hands to Heaven and prayed vociferously "Almighty Father" or "In the name of Jesus Christ," she must have had a direct line of communication to God because she was a very prosperous, kind, successful, respected, straightforward, and outspoken woman. She always put God first. She was a grassroots prayer warrior who approached every problem, challenge, and situation through assertive, soul-stirring prayer.

My other praying role model, Aunt D, is a meditative prayer warrior. She turns within and prays to God from the very depth of her center. Her prayer is strong, silent, and just as effective as Granny's. She is prosperous, contented, compassionate, beautiful, and very much at peace with life. We have an extremely close mother-daughter bond, and she is the most loving and giving person I've ever met in all my life.

Both these ladies taught me that prayer provides peace of mind.

Step Past the Petty Stuff and Go for a Higher Level of Understanding

To obtain peace of mind on Earth, we must achieve a balance among God, health, money, and love. When we get frustrated by life's challenges, we must not take it out on others. We must not be envious of what others have, or be sorrowful thinking of what we haven't got. When we become frustrated, we should think of the old, wise saying, "I felt sorry for myself because I didn't have any shoes—until I met the man who didn't have any feet."

A common source of frustration is other people's opposition to our opinions. We resent the people opposing us. We expect what we say to be accepted without question. But life doesn't work like that. Everyone has an individual opinion. In order to function, we must all be tactful and wise.

In order to move ahead in life, we must open ourselves to new ideas and concepts so that we can get along with other people. We need to entertain an open mind, regardless of how much we may know about a subject, because there is always more than one path to solve any problem.

It is helpful to criticize others and offer them useful suggestions if they ask for it. But we must break the habit of criticizing others unless doing so can help them. If your criticism serves no useful purpose, leave it alone. Try this experiment: Attempt to go just one full day without saying anything bad about anyone. See how rewarding you day will be.

There is enough space and wealth on the planet for everyone to enjoy the happy, beautiful, and fulfilling lives that God created us to have. Do not let anyone walk over you, but do not trample on anyone, either.

USE YOUR BODY AS A TEMPLE, NOT A TOMB

Instead of listening to, participating in, or falling prey to the negative spirit of idle gossip, evil thoughts, anger, prejudice, greed, guilt, malice, fear, or envy, let us make our body temples and homes into pleasant sanctuaries for God to dwell in.

Give your home a spiritual cleansing, and give your body a spiritual bath. Clean everything—throw out the clutter, excess paper, old clothes, malicious gossip, and bad company. Do a "spiritual spring cleaning" today. Use the spiritual gifts that the wise men presented to the baby Jesus—frankincense and myrrh. Buy them in liquid form, as essential oils. Pour some into a bucket of soapy water, and mop your floors and wipe your walls. Ask God to bless your home. Put a few drops in your bath water, and take a relaxing bubble bath. Ask God to bless your body.

Sis, it is most important to do a thorough internal spiritual body cleansing through praying and emptying out bad thoughts and deeds. Ask God to give you a bath in His spiritual bathtub. Remember, whatever goes around, comes around—the same concept as "whatever you sow, you will reap." The concept does not apply only to physical actions; it also holds true on the mental and spiritual planes. Whatever you think, your thought-vibrations will attract the same to you. The Law of Cause and Effect has boomerang action.

Once you have turned over a new leaf and evicted all the negative energy from your body temple, you'll feel very much at ease with yourself. The peace is so joyful and beautiful that I cannot find the words to describe it fully. It's a personal experience that each of us enjoys individually but equally. This is a promise from God, and it really works! Try it and see.

RENEW YOUR HOPE IN ORDER TO COPE

Sis, when the spirit of depression comes knocking at your door (and it will from time to time), do not let it in. Keep it out by filling yourself with positive affirmations and prayer. Surround yourself with positive friends, inspirational music, good books, lots of uplifting activities, and a really good church.

Sis, arm yourself with the spirit of God so that you will be protected and able to cope with any and every trial that may come your way. Just take it one day at a time. God promised, "I will not leave you comfortless; I will come to you." When the Comforter is in the house, a spiritual force field surrounds you, and a posted "do not enter" sign warns off all negative spirits—anxiety, frustration, depression, despondency, anger, compulsion, obsession, procrastination, neediness, rebellion, fear, jealousy. Whatever the negative spirit may be, it can have no power over you.

WE REAP WHAT WE SOW—BOTH THE GOOD AND THE BAD

How strong is your faith, sis? If you worship God only partially, you'll be blessed only partially. But if you pour all your heart into Him, without hesitation and fear, I promise you, you will reap the benefit of abundant blessings.

God knows our hearts—we cannot fool Him. Matthew 15:8 confirms, "This people draw near unto me with their mouths, and honor me with their lips, but their heart is far from me."

Too many people worship God with lip service only. Many false prophets only "talk the talk" and do not "walk the walk" of God. Here's a perfect example of someone who claims he is godly yet performed an ungodly act to the sister who wrote me this letter:

Dear Dr. Cornish,

I just read your book entitled *10 Bad Choices That Ruin Black Women's Lives* and found it to be excellent. But I need some direct advice about my situation. I am a twenty-nine-year-old senior at Boston University and will graduate in approximately two weeks. Prior to my college experience, I was in the U.S. Army for about seven years. I met and fell in love with Donald, who is now thirty-three years old.

When I met Donald (in May 1991), he and I were just friends. I had a boyfriend, and he had a fiancée (stationed overseas). We hung out as pals. My boyfriend cheated on me, and oddly enough so did Donald's fiancée. After a few months passed (in October 1991), we decided to date (which means that we became intimate). We soon found that this was too early for him, since he really was not over his former fiancée. He went overseas in December 1991 and returned to the States in April 1992. At this time, his former fiancée was in Memphis. He decided to go to Memphis to see her, and during that weekend she got pregnant. I was still very much in love with him and was hurt by all of this. They got married in July 1992 and the baby was born in December.

Donald and I remained friends (unfortunately more at times), and he separated from the army in May 1993. I was really happy to see him go because it meant that he was physically out of my life and that I no longer had to wrestle with my feelings about him. He and his wife separated in January 1994. I had kept in touch with him occasionally and knew what was going on in his life.

I decided to pursue a degree in broadcasting and separated from the army in July 1994. Donald and I got back together, and his divorce was finalized in April 1995. We have been dating since that time. He got a job in Maryland in September 1995 and moved there. I was going to school in Boston. We maintained a long-distance relationship through many trials. *He became an ordained minister in December 1997, and I thought that I could trust him.* He had grown and changed a great deal. Both of us decided to be celibate until we got married.

I need to take a minute to say that in 1996 he wanted to get married. I wanted to wait until I graduated. In 1997 I went through the "you (meaning he) need a degree in something" thing. He wasn't very stable, and I thought that he could use some direction; hence the degree. I worked through all of that because he has such a good heart and complements me so well that it became a nonissue.

A single attractive minister becomes great bait in any church, but especially in smaller ones. Each time I visited him in Maryland, it seemed as if a different woman were trying to become his "friend." The last time I was there, I got an extremely uneasy feeling about one woman in particular. I mentioned it to him, and he admitted that she really liked him but respected his position, so I really had nothing to worry about.

The next few months were very interesting. He became distant and canceled trips to see me, for one reason or another. Finally I decided to go to Maryland. The morning before I was to be there, he called me and confessed through tears that after one of our fights, he had cheated on me with the woman that I'd asked him about. I wanted to know if they were "dating." He said it was a one-time thing and that he didn't really know why it happened. I was completely devastated. *Here I am respecting him and all he is trying to be, and he does this!!!*

I demanded that he meet me halfway to discuss this further. He did, and we discussed this matter for about four hours. He confessed that he was insecure in our relationship. As long as I was in school, he did not feel as if I would meet anyone to whom I would be attracted. Now that I am going to graduate, he feels that I will meet my "equal" and realize that he doesn't measure up, and leave him all alone. He knows that I love him very much, and I do not say anything or treat him in any manner that would make him feel this way.

We decided to work through it. I told him that I wanted him to break all ties with this woman ASAP. He said he would start to make the necessary preparations to move to Boston, since trust would now become an issue. I agreed and promised to help him find an apartment once he found a job (or determined if he could transfer).

I expected to hear from him the following Monday. One of the terms of our agreement was that we communicate more and that he show remorse for what had happened. On Tuesday I called him at work. He said that he was going to call me the night before but did not have a calling card. He wanted to tell me about the conversation between him and the woman. I told him that as far as I was concerned, the only thing that he could say was that the friendship was over. He said he went to tell her that, and she told him that she was pregnant!!!!! I could have passed out! He said that while he had used a condom, there was some activity before he put it on (whatever that means).

Needless to say, I ended the relationship, but I still love him very much. He says that while he doesn't love this woman, he is considering marrying her to do "the right" thing. He feels as if he and she could make it work because of the baby. I am in shock. I never would have imagined that we would never be together again. Because we were friends first, I would like to end it that way, but I know that I cannot be his friend if he marries this woman.

I am not going to trash her because he was a willing party, but I really believe that she pulled one of the oldest tricks in the book, and she got him. Unfortunately, he was not strong enough to stand the test. What do you think? Can we be friends, or am I fooling myself? I am ashamed of this whole mess, but I really don't blame myself. He's been such a big part of my life for so long, I really do not know how to explain his absence. I will never tell my family what really happened. If you can offer any advice, I would really appreciate it.

Thank you,
Lisa

This Love Was Neither Anointed nor Appointed

My dear sister Lisa,

You have been through so much. I read your letter a few days ago, but I had to pray for you before I answered. Your story touched me deeply—I imagine, sis, that it must be doubly devastating for you to be deceived by someone who says he's of God. *This minister may be ordained by man, but he is not anointed by God.*

If he were God's anointed, he would not have led you on and lied to you; he would not have been sleeping with another woman when he agreed that you both would remain celibate until marriage; and he would certainly not have gotten her pregnant.

I agree with you that this woman used "the oldest trick in the book" to entrap him. But he had promised marriage to you—he should have kept his vow to you and to God. If he is not strong enough to live clean without cheating, he needs to find another profession. God's ministry is nothing to play around with. Donald may fool man and fool himself, but he can't fool God. He did a great wrong in the eyes of God. How unfortunate for him.

You deserve much better. This seems to be a behavior pattern for Donald. This is the second time in your long-term relationship that he has gotten another woman pregnant, chosen to marry her to "do the right thing," and left you to bear the pain on your own. It is obvious that he has not learned from his past mistake, where his first shotgun wedding ended in divorce. I urge you to learn from his track record—protect yourself and distance yourself from this confused man as soon as possible. It will hurt an awful lot. But once you get him out of your system, you will be much better off.

How foolish of him to use sex with another woman to boost his ego because he felt insecure about his relationship with you. If he felt "insecure," then as a person who believes in God (and especially a minister), he should have asked God for courage and confidence through prayer. If he cannot straighten out his own life properly, how in the world is he going to lead others to God?

I am very disgusted by this man's lies and cowardice. Sis, you know what—the Holy Spirit (and your intuition) will always reveal those who are not suitable for us. You have had a revelation twice about Donald. Let go. Turn to God, and ask for strength to ease the pain and hurt you are feeling. Please read Psalm 118 and know that God is watching over you, especially with this verse: "The stone which the builders have refused, is now become the head stone of the corner." Jesus confirmed this same fact in Mark 12:10 (and in Matthew 21:42).

You can write Donald a letter if you choose to, to clear out all the pain you have inside. Mail it, and let go. Your wounds are still too new. You will only be "pretending" to be friends, because you will be hurting too much. Maybe somewhere down the line, but in the meantime, take care of you. Be the best you can be, so in the right time, you will attract the right person. One who really cares about you; one who really deserves you.

Congratulations on your graduation. Please take care of your-self, and keep in touch from time to time. May God bless you.

Sincerely,

Dr. Grace Cornish

RELIGION WITHOUT SPIRITUAL KINDNESS IS FALSE

Sis, make sure when you share your heart with a man, you do so with to a *spiritual* man, one who has the spirit of God in him. Even if he happens to be a *religious* man, make sure that he also has the spirit of God in him. Because anyone can religiously lie, religiously cheat, or religiously fool you. The Bible says, "The let-ter killeth, but the *spirit* giveth life."

Donald is obviously not yet ready to be a dedicated leader in the ministry. His "spirit may be willing, but his flesh is weak." So many awesome and wonderful ministers, pastors, preachers, and church leaders have the true anointing of the Lord and help to lead, heal, guide, direct, redirect, and uplift people's lives. I truly admire, appreciate, and respect these genuine and dedicated men (and women) of God.

Unfortunately, there are also many fake "ministers" who go into the church as a business, not as a calling. But God will not be mocked—He will deal with them at the appropriate time.

It is important to develop your very own personal relationship with God, so that you will not be misled by any of the false prophets who are running rampant today. Please, get into a good church, with an anointed minister who has the spirit of the Lord in him or her, and worship there in fellowship, joy, and thanks-giving.

"THE LETTER KILLETH, BUT THE SPIRIT GIVETH LIFE"

Sis, ask God to bless you with a discerning spirit to determine and get rid of everything false in your life: false beliefs, false goals, false pride, false friends, false relationships, and false leaders.

Overall, you find many more women in church than men. There is a great imbalance here—many men at the pulpit, yet few in the pew. Where are the majority of our brothers hiding out on Sundays?

It is unfortunate but true that some men are waiting until after they have sown all their wild oats and are approaching fifty; or until their backs are bent and their bodies are afflicted with illness; or until they can hardly walk or can barely stay awake between sentences. Then and only then do they choose to drag their carcasses to God (and to a committed relationship with one woman). Sis, don't be a last resort for any man. Jeremiah 31:22 asks, "How long wilt thou go about, O thou backsliding daughter? For the Lord hath created a new thing in the earth, a woman shall compass a man."

Sis, a compass guides and gives direction. Please "compass" the men in your life toward God. It doesn't have to be a lover, husband, or mate. It could be a friend, coworker, or stranger. We are our brother's keepers. It is the worst thing to see someone die without having God in his or her life. Seeing a twenty-seven-year-old brother struggle for his last breath was one of the most life-changing and eye-opening experiences I have ever had.

LIFE IS FULL OF THE UNEXPECTED—ALWAYS BE SPIRITUALLY ALERT

In February 1997 I was at a health spa in La Ceiba, Honduras. I went there for a month to work on *10 Bad Choices That Ruin Black Women's Lives.* It is very peaceful and quiet. In the cottage next to mine was a nurturing fifty-four-year-old mother from Connecticut, Celia, and her son, Richard.

Richard was very handsome, six foot one with chiseled features. Sadly, however, this young brother weighed only ninety-eight pounds. His immune system had broken down—his body was invaded by the AIDS virus. Richard had become a human skeleton, purely skin and bones. Everything else had been eaten away by this destructive disease. His body was so far gone that medical doctors had already written him off as deceased. They informed Celia that it was just "a matter of a few weeks."

Celia, a loving mother who would do anything for her four children, had transported Richard, her third child, to La Ceiba in desperate hopes that the natural herbs, pollution-free air, invigorating sulfur saunas, and hot mineral spring baths would help to regenerate him.

It did help a little, because Richard did not die in a "few weeks" as foretold. He had already been at La Celia for about three months when I got there. Celia and I became friends. On my way to the sauna house in the mornings, I would pass by their cottage to say hello. Celia would be spoon-feeding Richard, cleaning him, or changing the diapers he had to wear. Some days she would lift his body, place him in a wheelchair, and take him outside to get some sun and fresh air. Other days she would beg him to try to eat something, because he had lost his appetite. Many days he was unable to digest his food and would throw it up. Celia would clean him right away.

Celia was tired, but her deep love for her child kept her going. She never shrugged off her responsibility. She talked with me every day to help renew her strength and stay hopeful.

At first it was difficult and painful for me to look at Richard's frail body, which had collapsed like a pile of putty onto the bed to which he was anchored. But I prayed and asked God to put away my own fears and use me to help where I could.

Richard had some bad days and some no-so-bad days. One morning Celia told me that he had said he was determined to live—and that he would be up and about by the summer. It brought tears to my eyes. Every day I would visit him to try and cheer him up: "Yo, Richard, how are you today, my handsome brother? Make sure you get well soon so I can take you out on a date." He nodded and smiled. And his mother laughed and cried—she was so happy to see her son smile.

Some days he was in excruciating pain, but he kept hanging on. Then one Sunday evening, about eight o'clock, I was in my cottage, lying on the bed in an oversize T-shirt, praying, and reading my Bible. I had been meditating and praying for about two hours, when I heard a pounding and a desperate cry at the door. When I got up and opened it, Celia was standing there, tears streaming down her cheeks. "Grace, can you come and help me?" she gasped. "I don't think Richard is going to make it through the night."

GOD CALLS YOU WHEN YOU LEAST EXPECT IT

My heart leaped. "Okay, I'll be right there," I promised. "Let me just put on some leggings."

As I pulled on the leggings as quickly as I could, my heart was pounding—I was panicking. I kept praying, "Oh God, please let him be okay. Please don't let him die now. . . . What can I do, Lord? Please help me here, guide me, use me. . . . Do whatever you need to do, but just take charge and help us here. Oh, Lord . . ."

I heard a voice as clear as day say, "Calm down, and be at peace. Take your Bible and go right now." It was as if I were dreaming; but this was no dream.

I obeyed immediately. I can't explain what happened, but a peaceful calm swept through me. With my Bible in hand, I went to the cottage next door. Celia ran to me, crying, "Grace, he's not going to make it, my baby is not going to make it."

"Ssshhh . . . don't let Richard hear you say that. It may upset him," I whispered. "Let us try to comfort him." (She had already called for the doctor who owned the health spa, but he had not shown up.)

I looked in the direction of Richard's bed. He was just lying there, his eyes closed, his body almost lifeless—except that he kept grinding his teeth and making these painful sounds. It sounded like a poor, helpless animal caught in a trap, struggling to get free, and screaming for help in a deep-seated growl. It sounded like *"RRRRRRrrrrr, RRRRRRrrrrr..."* The sounds were wild, sharp, and piercing.

I walked over and sat in a chair next to his bed and placed the Bible on his nightstand. Richard kept grinding his teeth, and the growls kept getting louder. They would suddenly cease for a few minutes, then start up again. I tried comforting him, "It's okay, Richard. You're not alone. It's going to be okay." The grinding of the teeth and the growls kept getting louder and sharper.

I read Psalm 91 and sang the hymn "Anointing Fall on Me." The song seemed to soothe him because the grinding and growling sounds lowered. So I sang the same song over and over and over. Every time I stopped to rest my throat, Richard's sounds would grow louder. Then I continued singing, "Let the power of the Holy Ghost fall on me; anointing fall on me," and it would soothe him again. This went on for about four hours straight. By this time, poor Celia was at her wit's end. She sat on the other bed across the room and just kept crying, "Oh God, my baby, my baby, my baby." She had called for the doctor a few more times, but he was nowhere to be found.

At about midnight, Richard let out the most excruciating growl I've ever heard. It startled both Celia and me. I leaped out of the chair and stood next to the upper half of his body. Celia flew from where she was sitting and stood by the lower half. At the top of her lungs, she cried out, "Oh God, he's dying! My Richard is dying!"

The louder Richard ground his teeth and growled, the louder Celia would scream and cry. Trying to comfort Richard, and trying to calm Celia at the same time, drained energy from my body, but I was compelled to keep going. The noise coming out of Richard was so loud that it echoed off the walls. He was tormented; his eyelids kept fluttering up and down. In a daze, I whispered to God, "What is going on here? How can such an army of noise be coming out of such a frail body? Father, what must I do now? Please tell me what to do."

GOD IS ALWAYS IN CHARGE—SEEK HIS GUIDANCE

I was guided to pray for Richard. By now, Celia was screaming hysterically. "Celia, please, you've got to help me now," I pleaded. "This is not crying time, this is praying time." A calm and peaceful spirit returned to me once again. "Celia, don't fear. If it's not Richard's time to go, God will heal him. But if it is his time, he needs to pass in peace. If you keep screaming, it will not help him. We have got to pray for him together."

Celia fell silent, and we knelt by his bedside together. I prayed, and Celia wept. As Richard's growls subsided to groans, he started gasping for breath. Tears were streaming down his cheeks. I reached over, hugged him, and comforted him as if he were my own son. "Richard, there is nothing to be afraid of," I kept assuring him, "God loves you. If He doesn't want you to leave here now, nothing is going to happen to you. Your mother loves you, and she is here beside you. But if it's your time to leave, you're not alone, God will send an angel to guide and protect you."

This went on for about two hours. At two o'clock that Monday morning, Richard let out a final gasp. His body went limp in my arms.

I stared at the lifeless body before me. "God, is this it?" I asked. "What happened? Where did the energy go that kept this body working? Did it go up, down, in, out? Where is it, Father? Was his spirit in that last gasp that escaped from his mouth? Isn't this the same body that was just breathing a few seconds ago? Make me understand, Lord."

It was as if someone had just flipped a switch to "off" and shut down his engine in a split second. Poor Celia screamed and wailed in agony, "My son is dead, oh, God, my baby is dead."

"No, Celia—he isn't," I said. "Richard isn't dead. His body is dead, but his spirit is alive. His body had deteriorated so badly that his spirit couldn't dwell there anymore. So it evacuated. Richard's mind was trying to hold on, but his physical body was too far gone. The spirit is what gives us life, but it cannot remain in a very sick body for long. When it leaves us, our physical machinery shuts down. God, the giver of life, is a spirit, so we have to worship Him in the spirit—to make sure that when it is time for our spirits to leave our body temples, they will go directly back to God. Let us pray together that Richard's spirit is now at peace and has found its way back to God."

Celia and I leaned on each other's shoulders, hugged, wept, and prayed.

YOUR LIFE IS WORTH LIVING TO THE FULLEST— RIGHT NOW, SIS

When I returned home, I was on the phone one evening with Norman, one of my closest friends. I shared the experience of Richard's passing with him. "Norman," I asked, "why do you think God has made me see death so close?"

"Maybe He wants you to testify to others what you've learned from these experiences," Norman responded. "You should use it to help other people's lives."

I took his advice, and in *10 Bad Choices That Ruin Black Women's Lives,* I openly shared with readers the story of seeing my natural mother murdered in front of me when I was ten years old. And now I share Richard's death here. Here is the spiritual lesson I learned:

It took death to teach me about living—truly living, and enjoying the gift of life. I prayed that my mother's soul would be at peace. Her death and Richard's both affected me so strongly that they caused me to seek the meaning of our time on Earth. I searched for some positive message I could give to my own precious daughter, my mate, and my family—and to you, your mate, your children, and your family. I meditated and prayed. I dedicate this prayer to my mother's and Richard's memories:

THE GIFT OF LIFE

Life is a gift from God. Each human being is given an individual personality and free will. Each of us is given the chance to create our individual story. Each must have a personal relationship with our Father, the Creative Life Force.

Our purpose is to become one with God, to see beyond the veil that clouds our minds, to learn to listen to the still voice within. The kingdom of God is within each of us. All we need to do is desire and look, and we shall discover it.

Life comes with many tests and challenges. The earth is a gigantic school. We are each placed in various classrooms to learn and grow. Passing these tests depends on our individual wills and application. To know is not enough. We must not simply take in words—we must be willing to *apply* ourselves in God-thought, God-action, and God-deed. This does not mean becoming docile and letting anyone walk over us, but being compassionate and respectful of others' right to *be*.

Sure, many are devious in their thoughts and actions, but we must be wise enough to avoid being used, abused, or ensnared by these lost ones. Let that be their karma, not ours. We must be harmless in our application of Universal Laws. The Law of Cause and Effect shares, "Whatever goes around, comes around."

In life we must share, but not so much of ourselves that we lose ourselves, nor so little that we become selfish. It is a balance—a Christ Consciousness balance. This balance we must all find within; then we can truly live a full life.

We are all born and die in the Earth. This is part of God's plan. It doesn't matter into which situation we were born—what matters is how we use what we have today to progress on God's path. Our individual destiny lies within each of individual soul. Each of us must make our personal approach to the Life Force (God).

The life of our individual soul is continuous. We have the same soul yesterday, today, and tomorrow. Our whole purpose is to get the soul to become one with our Maker; and we'll keep learning the lessons until we get them right.

The past is already gone. What's important is how we choose to live and love today. Our Father is a very kind and forgiving God. We can be forgiven of all our past mistakes if we sincerely want to be and simply ask to be. But we must genuinely let go of all past hurts, ill feelings, and bad memories of people and of ourselves. Condemning ourselves is just as sinful as condemning others.

To live life fully is to discover and develop the Christ Consciousness in each of us. It is to acknowledge our Creator, and to love Him with our entire beings, because He is our entire being. It is to respect and be kind to others and treat them as we wish to be treated; to let go of blockages and simply love our lives and the existence of people. If we know a scorpion will sting us, however, we wouldn't embrace it in our bosoms. So embrace not those individuals who choose to walk away from the Light, but pray for them, and release them from your consciousness.

The gift of life is to create a worthwhile and purposeful existence. Living the will of God fulfills this purpose. Whatever we choose to do or become is our individual birthright, as long as we focus on the Creator. We can choose to become as rich, prosperous, and successful as we desire, as long as we do so without harming or robbing others. Being happy and enjoying the richness of the Earth is a gift from God. We must constantly ask ourselves, "How do I choose to be written in the Book of Life?"

The gift of life gives us the opportunity to bask in the beauty of the Earth. The key to unlocking this fullness is in the essence of each of us—this is God's doing. Not a god that is fictitious, distorted, made out of stone, or misrepresented, but the Living God, the God that is real—very real—within the very center of those who genuinely choose to find Him. "Seek and ye shall find; ask and it shall be given; knock and it shall be open unto you."

The Kingdom of God is not necessarily or exclusively found in any pope, preacher, or building. But the Kingdom is within the body temples of all who choose to let God in: "I stand at the door and knock, and if ye will open, I will come in and sup with thee."

Life and death are interchangeable transitions in God's plan for us. They are mirror images, reflections of each other. Life is what we are at this moment, so let us live it—live it in the way of God.

With God, there is no fear, guilt, hatred, selfishness, or envy. There is instead love, wisdom, kindness, understanding, and peace of mind. With this gift of peace, we can face each day with hope, optimism, and enthusiasm to go about our business in the present moment.

When the beauty and strength of the Christ Consciousness becomes our new consciousness, then we can truly appreciate and understand the cycle of life without fear. At any moment, hour, or day God moves us on by the experience we call death, all He is doing is transporting us through His other door—until He decides it's our time to be resurrected for everlasting life with Him.

To sum it up neatly, you are a three-dimensional creation. God has blessed you with a mind, body, and spirit: "The spirit gives you life, the mind constructs your life, and the physical is the outcome of your life."

Use all three wisely.

EXERCISE YOUR RIGHT TO COCREATE WITH THE CREATOR

We have no control over when we come into this world or when we leave. But we have been given the gift to cocreate our individual lives while we are now on the planet. Mother Teresa, the Roman Catholic nun who inspired millions with her absolute devotion to the world's dispossessed, once said, "Each of us is merely a small instrument; all of us, after accomplishing our mission, will disappear."

Sis, it is our responsibility to ourselves, and to our Creator, to fulfill the individual purpose for which we were incarnated on Earth. That purpose is to love our Creator, love ourselves, and love our fellow human beings, regardless of race, nationality, or form. If we dislike anyone, it should be only because that person has a specific behavior or mannerism that may be harmful to us. Otherwise, we must strive to relieve suffering and to bring joy to friends and strangers alike.

A true test of love is how we treat our neighbors. People claim they love God, and God told us to love our fellow human beings. So if people don't love their fellow man, then how can they love God? The love they claim is hypocritical.

All human beings are born with the natural instinct to love. Somewhere along our life-path, from childhood through adulthood, this instinct is often abused, mistreated, or unappreciated by a parent, friend, lover, or stranger. This can make us cautious and distrustful of others and unappreciative of ourselves. In order to survive the hurt and pain we feel, we build protective coatings around our hearts.

Our hearts are the center of love. Love is life's natural medicine. We must release the healing power of love in order to have healthy relationships with others. We must treat others with the level of respect that we would like to be treated with.

ALWAYS PRAY TO FIND THE BEST WAY

In October 1998, I did a discussion and book signing for *10 Bad Choices That Ruin Black Women's Lives* at Borders in the World Trade Center. It was a very pleasant evening, with about seventy-five men and women present.

I really enjoy doing these seminars, simply because I love the work I do. I usually focus on solving unhealthy issues between men and women. I have never tried to force my personal belief and closeness to God and Christ in the seminars, even though I *always* pray quietly to God right before each one: "Heavenly Father, I humble myself before you. I give myself to you as an empty vessel for you to use as you please. Fill me up with your Holy Spirit that I may give hope, peace, understanding, comfort, and joy to everyone who seeks help today. Thank you, your daughter, Grace."

The discussion at Borders progressed beautifully. During the question-and-answer portion, participants and I exchanged some useful and terrific information. At one point, a well-groomed, thirtysomething brother asked, "Dr. Cornish, you are very spiritual, aren't you?"

"Yes, I am." I smiled. "What made you ask?"

"I can just tell. Your face, your personality, and your presence are so warm and friendly," he replied. "Can you tell us how important it is to have spirituality in a relationship, or do you think it's important at all?"

"It is definitely important," I answered. "We are three-dimensional creations with minds, bodies, and spirits. If we do not bond with all three components in relationships, then at some point those relationships are bound to fail. But if two people first meet spirit to spirit, then direct their minds and bodies to work together in natural harmony, they experience a most rewarding and fascinating bonding that mere words cannot describe. This is what people are really longing for when they say they want to meet a *soul mate*—it's really *a spirit mate* that they're looking for."

The audience applauded my explanation. This opened the path to further discussion about the connection between life, love, spirituality, and God. I shared some of the good choices discussed in this book, and I shared the spiritual life-lessons that I learned from Richard's and my mother's deaths. The discussion was supposed to end at eight o'clock, but it just kept going because people wanted to know more. A very articulate sister in the audience asked, "Dr. Cornish, how do you keep your faith so strong?"

"Through prayer, sis," I responded. "I use 'praying power' for 'staying power.' It is very important that each individual form his or her own personal relationship with God. Don't take anybody's word at face value—seek the truth for yourself. Even if someone tells you something that seems convincing, go and isolate yourself with God and pray for His truth. He will reveal *His truth* to you through your prayers. I pray about everything. Even if you don't understand or fully believe, pray, 'Lord, please help me. I have a hard time believing because I don't know what the truth is. Can you please show me what *you* want me to do?'"

GET INTO GOD, SO GOD CAN GET INTO YOU

Don't ever think you're too sophisticated or advanced to humble yourself before God, I explained. "Education minus God equals confusion. So many people wait until pain really hits them, or until they become very sick, and then they cry, 'Oh God, please help me!' Now, if you decide to do so, that's your personal choice, but you will be shortchanging yourself. Get to God at some point in your life, the sooner the better. God is the Giver of life, so make sure you relate to Him and thank Him for your precious life."

At nine I closed the discussion on a spiritually high note and prepared to sign the books. About sixty people assembled in line. I greeted everyone personally as I signed their copies.

About halfway through the line, I was signing a book for a woman in her mid-thirties, when she said to me, "I agreed with almost every thing you said except when you said that 'God is a forgiving God, and He will accept us if we pray.' It's a lie, because we are all sinners and we will all die as sinners and end up in hell."

"Pardon me?" I said

"I said we are all sinners and will die and go to hell," she repeated.

"If that's what you believe, then that's what you believe. Everyone is entitled to his or her own opinion," I said politely.

"It's not my opinion. It's the truth. It's in the Bible," she blurted out. "And what you said about God forgiving us is wrong."

"I don't know what you've been reading," I told her, "but if you don't think that God is a forgiving God, then that's your personal choice, sis."

"It's not my choice," she argued. "God hates sinners, and we are all sinners."

People on line were getting impatient and wanted her to move along. Since she insisted on being heard, I asked her to step to the side until I signed the remaining books. Then I would be able to speak with her some more.

"PATIENCE IS TRULY A VIRTUE"

She sat on a chair about ten feet away from me. About nine other people were sitting in the area. She said loud enough for me to hear, "I'm going to get her now. I'll set her straight. How can she tell people that they can speak to God directly? It's a lie."

I glanced up and smiled at her and said, "Don't worry, I'm going to give you some attention as soon as I finish signing these books. In the meantime, try to be at peace, sis." By this time, she was huffing and puffing.

When I finished, I beckoned to her. "Come talk to me. What's the problem?" I asked.

She kept raising her voice, as if she were a time bomb getting ready to explode. "We are sinners," she said, "and demons are loose on the earth. They are taking us over, and we will die in sin. God won't change that."

"What is wrong with you?" a sister asked her.

"Which church do you go to?" a brother wanted to know.

She ignored them and kept her attention and anger focused on me. "God don't forgive sins. People on the Earth are fallen angels, and we are all going to go to hell."

"Sis, take it easy, relax," I said. "There's no need to carry on like this. If you raise your voice, I will not speak with you. Now, let us reason in a civilized manner."

I told her about the four gospels, God's love for us, the teachings of Jesus, and the works of Peter, Paul, and other spiritual teachers in the New Testament. She was baffled. She had obviously never read any of the New Testament. Yet each time she caught herself absorbing the information, she snapped back to her original oratory about hell and damnation. When she couldn't logically dispute what I was teaching her, she just hollered even louder about "the weakness of sinners, the strength of demons, and the home of hell."

Oddly, this sister didn't appear to be some scatterbrain or crazy person. She seemed to be a bright woman who unfortunately had been brainwashed into believing that she, and everyone else, had a personal space reserved for them in hell.

BE FIRM, STAND STILL, AND LET THE SPIRIT OF GOD GUIDE YOU

"You better step out of that dead mess and get into life," I told her. "I didn't invent the promise of God's love and forgiveness. These are not my words—they are written right there in the Bible. We are in a bookstore. If you don't believe me, then go and get a Bible from one of the shelves, and I'll show you word for word everything I have told you."

I couldn't have said that soon enough for her. She was so eager to prove me wrong that she dashed off and returned only a few minutes later, waving a King James version triumphantly in the air. "Go ahead," she smirked. "I bet you can't prove any of that stuff you claimed."

"Take it easy, sis. Be still," I replied as I opened the Bible. It's truly fascinating how the spirit of God moves. After a quick silent prayer—*Father, please guide my hands, and take me where you want me to go*—I didn't even have to search through the pages. As if an unseen hand were helping me, I turned to the exact page I needed at the exact moment. Each page I went to showed a scripture to back up what I had shared with the sister and to contradict every negative thing she had said. People around us were amazed, and some kept saying, "Wow, I didn't know that. You're so good."

"It's not me," I said. "It's the love of God here tonight. It's His words that are good. And He is for everyone who chooses to believe in Him."

I explained to the sister that I realized where she was coming from, but that her understanding and belief were not completed. She had been taught only the Old Testament and nothing of the New Testament. "God had a strong bond with man when He created him in the beginning of time," I shared. "But because of man's sin, it separated him from God. At many times in the past, God regretted that He had made man. Genesis 6:5–6 says, 'And God saw the wickedness of man was great in the earth, and that every imagination of the thoughts of his heart was only evil continually. And it repented the Lord that he had made man on earth, and it grieved him at his heart.'" But, I added, "this was before the New Testament.

"The New Testament is a new covenant between God and man," I added. The Cross represents the reconciliation, the meeting between God and man—the spirit of God coming down to earth, and the spirit of man being lifted up, both meeting at the crossroads."

I don't know how much time had passed, but it must have been about an hour or so, because one of the staff announced that the store would be closing in half an hour. The sister's demeanor appeared to be soothed by the scriptures I read to her, but believe it or not, she went right back to speaking extremely loud and admonishing, "We are all sinners and God is not going to save us."

SIS, DO NOT LET NEGATIVE PEOPLE WEAR YOU OUT

The people around us shook their heads in disbelief. I was getting tired and realized that it was time to close the conversation. "I have shown you scriptures written in the Bible to counteract every negative belief you have thrown out. You have never read any of the New Testament, and that's why you don't expect to reap any of the benefits. Sis, you're missing out on a beautiful treasure. Now, before you argue against it any further, at least read it, so that when and if you challenge it again, you can at least debate it logically. If you want to believe that you are 'a sinner and will die as one,' that's up to you, sis. I'm not here to criticize you for your belief. But please do not try to force your outdated concept on me, because I will not accept it."

"But you said that people can stop demons and bad energy from taking over their bodies," she retaliated in an offensively loud voice. "That's a lie. We don't have that power."

FORWARD EVER, BACKWARD NEVER

"Sure we do. I'm going to exercise my power right now. You are trying to drain my energy, and I will not let you do it. I have been here with you for over an hour. Enough already," I declared. "I don't know why you're so angry and yelling so rudely. Who put that stuff in your mind? They have you believing that you are not worthy of God's love and that you are subjected to demons—the demons of anger, depression, fear, guilt, envy, illness, confusion—and that's wrong. It's all backward. You've got to move forward in life and get with the program—the resurrection program. But because you are so angry and so stuck in your negative beliefs, there's no getting through to you right now.

"At some point you should read and try to understand the story about how Jesus cast out the demonic legion. It is recorded in three gospels: Matthew 8:28–34, Mark 5:1–19, and Luke 8:26–37. Jesus was entering a city, and he met a possessed man coming out of the tombs. No one could pass by the demoniac because he was exceedingly vicious, and not even chains could bind him. But when Jesus walked by, the possessed man fell down and begged him, 'Jesus thou son of the Living God, please don't torment me.'

"The demoniac knew that Jesus had the power of God operating through Him. Jesus asked, 'What is your name?' It replied, 'Legion. For we are many.'

"'Hold your peace and come out of him,' Jesus commanded. In other words, 'Shut up and get lost.' There is not a demon-possessed person on this entire planet who can stand up to the power of God in action. We don't have to go around casting out demons, but we must protect ourselves from falling prey to negative energy and negative people. There are many demonic and evil-thinking people in the world today. They have come for a purpose—the murders, drugs, child pornography, and sexual orgies are nothing short of demonic energy. But none can harm you if you wrap yourself in the spiritual protection of God because 'greater is He that is in you, than He that is in the world.'"

THE SPIRIT OF THE LORD IS A WONDER-WORKING SPIRIT

People need to believe in God and get energized, I explained to the sister, and take authority over any and all negative forces in their households, their families, and their husbands' and children's lives. "Too many husbands are straying, and too many schoolchildren are on drugs, selling their bodies, and fighting their parents. Parents especially have to stand spiritually firm. If a child has been taken over by drugs or corruption, get some professional help, but more importantly, lean over that child's body, even when he is asleep at night, and get into some serious good old-fashioned grassroots prayer to spiritually cleanse that child."

REBUKE THE NEGATIVE FORCES FROM YOUR SURROUNDINGS

At this point, the sister in Borders yelled at the top of her voice, "We will all die in sin." I shook my head because I felt sorry her and said, "I don't know what your personal gripe is, sis, but please go home and pray to God, and ask Him for His personal guidance."

She kept trying to object, but I stood firm, "Sis, I'm not going to finance your negative energy with any more of my positive energy tonight. I can feel you trying to pull energy from me. This conversation is now closed. Now go and pray and ask God to reveal His truth to you. He does love you, and He will answer you, regardless of what anyone else has told you to the contrary."

She stormed away, still yelling. I felt deeply troubled that that sister's mind was so confused and programmed with defeat. But I couldn't help her anymore that night. Her anger and loudness had exhausted me. I wouldn't allow her to pull me any further onto her negative spiritual battleground.

It's both frightening and sad that people's lives are just slipping away day by day without any kind of joy, peace, or hope. I went home and prayed deeply for this sister. Wherever she is, may God's loving spirit melt the hardness surrounding her heart and the harshness tormenting her mind.

Sis, please don't let anyone, or any institution, or any group brainwash you. Find God for yourself. God will bless you favorably if you choose to let Him into your spirit, heart, and mind. Pray, and give thanks in advance for your blessings.

YOU ARE INDEED GOD'S RARE ROSE, SIS!

Well, sis, we have come to the closing words in your guide for creating balance among God, health, money, and love. In the introduction to this book, I promised that you would experience some fantastic and amazing changes by the time you got to this point—

and I'm sure you have. Please write and tell me about some of them: P.O. Box 4739, New York, New York 10185-0040.

One of the most important lessons you can take away from this empowerment guide is "Form your own personal and unique relationship with God." In Jeremiah 29:13, He promised, "You shall seek me, and find me *when* you shall search for me with all your heart."

Seek Him so you can find Him, sis. You are my sister, and I care about your life. Here's wishing you a beautiful, prosperous, happy, healthy, and empowered life. May God bless you always.

This may be the end of this book, but it is only the beginning of your new, enchanting, and empowered life. You deserve happiness, sis. *Go for it—with God's blessing!*

about the author

Dr. Grace Cornish is well known to millions of TV viewers for her down-to-earth, highly effective advice on TV shows like *FOX on Family, WOR-TV News, Montel Williams, Ricki Lake, Good Day New York,* and *FOX-TV News.* She is the "After-care Psychologist" for the *Queen Latifah Show.*

A well-traveled motivational speaker, businesswoman, and seminar leader, with a Ph.D. in social psychology, Dr. Grace has charmed and inspired audiences in the United States, England, France, Switzerland, and Jamaica with her delivery of positive messages of self-worth directed to women and men from all walks of life.

As an author, she has packed her many years of experience as an image consultant and relationship therapist into three books of self-empowerment—*The Fortune of Being Yourself* (also published in Spanish); *Think and Grow Beautiful* (designed for teenage readers); and *Radiant Women of Color* (a Barnes & Noble best-seller).

Her current best-seller, *10 Bad Choices That Ruin Black Women's Lives,* is published by Crown.

Dr. Grace served as the advice columnist for the *New York Beacon* weekly newspaper and *Belle* magazine. She has been featured in many of the nation's leading print and broadcast media. In the course of her career, Dr. Grace has received a number of honors, including recognition by Who's Who in America, Who's Who in the East, and Who's Who in Writers, Editors and Poets.

You can visit her Web site at www.drcornish.com.

GOOD NEWS TRAVELS FAST!

You can arrange to bring Dr. Grace's "10 Good Choices" empowerment seminar to your area. To book Dr. Grace Cornish for keynote speeches, seminars, workshops, lectures, and retreats, please contact her speaking agent:

Brian Manaco
Worldwide Talent Group, LTD
537 Steamboat Road
Greenwich, CT 06830

(203) 625-5583
Fax: (203) 625-0190
E-mail: WTGroup@aol.com

Here's what people are saying about Dr. Grace's seminars:

"Back by popular demand, Dr. Cornish is an empowering speaker you won't want to miss!"
    Barnes & Noble

"When the Doctor is in, she draws a crowd."
    The Atlanta Daily

"This lady has a knack for inspiring people."
    The Sunday Herald

"We keep inviting Dr. Grace back because she's simply the best!"
    "Good Day, New York"